P9-BZO-881

95

BANNERS
and Such

by
ADELAIDE ORTEGEL, SP

Published by
RESOURCE PUBLICATIONS, INC.
160 E. Virginia St.
San Jose, CA 95112

Editorial Director: Kenneth Guentert
Production Editor: Scott Alkire
Designer and Illustrator: Adelaide Ortegel, SP
Photographs: Robert Wells

ISBN 0-89390-092-3
Printed and bound in the United States 5 4 3 2 1
Revised edition, 1986. Copyright © 1986 by Adelaide Ortegel, SP. All rights reserved. For
reprint permission, write to Resource Publications, Inc., 160 E. Virginia St., #290, San Jose,
CA 95112.

IN GOD'S OWN IMAGE WE CREATE

We are made in the image and likeness of God.
God's Presence in the world is an on-going creation.

BANNERS AND SUCH is offered as an invitation and a help
for you and others to continue the work of creation.

TO CREATE...TO CELEBRATE...is to be fully alive, to take
the gift of life and live it with meaning.
A banner is meant to be a celebration. It proclaims the
hopes and dreams, joys or sorrows of a faith community.

a drop of WONDER

catch it! shout it's cool sparkle

bursting in on you

To communicate this WONDER-BURSTING is the journey of
                                          becoming human.

THE JOURNEY IS...

BEING YOURSELF

Each person is gifted in a special way. The GIFT is the
unique, unrepeatable EVENT of life each of us is in the
world.
Being CREATIVE is being yourself,
    discovering the sources of your own uniqueness,

        probing, sometimes with laughter,
                    sometimes with tears,
                what makes you, YOU

        building on your own thoughts, ideas, dreams

        trying new techniques, unlikely combinations

        letting the materials and tools express what
                they can do within YOUR imagination

        freeing yourself from the familiar to launch
                out into untried ways.

TO RISK

CREATIVE ACTIVITY is an adventure.
It may put you in a precarious position,
    but the growing edge is always into the UNKNOWN.

TO STRUGGLE

Sometimes you have to wrestle with words or ideas...
        BREAKING THEM OPEN in order to find out
                        what they really mean.
The STRUGGLE is the process of pulling all the parts
                together into wholeness.

OVER THE LONG HAUL

CREATIVITY calls for sustained effort
                            if newness is to grow.
The seedling, pushing its way up through hard soil, is
in slow, delicate process. With the right environment it
will grow and blossom into something beautiful which can
be shared.

6

Part 1   A LOOK AT CREATIVITY

What happens when CREATIVITY is stirred?
How is it nurtured?
What are the stages of growth?

CREATIVITY is free and dynamic. It happens
differently for different people, but there
are certain characteristic styles of involve-
ment that become apparent. An understanding
of the process will help you enable creative
growth to take place.

JOY OF DISCOVERY

EXPLORING
GATHERING ideas and experiences
BECOMING sensitized
EXPERIMENTING with materials
TRYING new combinations

CREATING does not happen in a vacuum. It grows from rich
experiences and requires an environment of trust and accep-
tance. There needs to be opportunity for letting your ideas
and imagination enjoy the freedom of surprise. As people
start experimenting with materials they forget self-conscious
hesitancy and begin sharing in the excitement of trying new
things. The first DISCOVERY may be simply what fun it is to
give new shape to things. The finished or unfinished pro-
ducts should be appreciated for what they are...
JOYOUS BEGINNINGS!

Here's an example:

*At St. Mary-of-the-Woods, Indiana, a group of one
hundred teachers had participated in four intensive days
designed to sharpen sensory awareness. They had explored
sound and movement, had gathered fragrances and tastes,
had begun to SEE in new ways. It was the morning of the
fifth day -- a journey into creating. Each person was
given a small piece of self-hardening clay. We were
gathering for a walk through the woods to another building. The clay was meant to be a tactile, sensitizing
medium as well as an invitation to create. I suggested
that they look for tools along the way.*

*We started out in a spirit of fun and laughter, led by
the music of a recorder group. Clay became snakes and rab-
bits and funny faces. When the clay started to dry out,
some people moistened it in the dew on the grass or in a
drinking fountain. Little by little people became more involved in their clay. They began pressing the clay into
the textures all around them. Tiny stones, twigs, bark,
became a part of the clay creations.*

*The final touches were added as everyone came together
in the assembly room. The clay objects were carefully
placed in the sun to dry. By this time they were no longer lumps of clay, but very personal shapings of that cool
morning walk.*

SUGGESTIONS for ENABLING DISCOVERY

EXPLORING
Take a look at your own immediate environment as if
you had never seen it before. Look for unusual bits
of life -- pieces that make your world.

GATHERING ideas and experiences
Search out the needs and concerns within the group.
Listen honestly to your own feelings and the feelings
of others.
Take time to talk with strangers. Be open to the
energy and risk of new viewpoints.
Share glimpses of human-ness and meaning -- moments
of celebration.

BECOMING sensitized
Try to remove the blinders that cut you off from a
full view of life.
Use a slide mount frame to focus in and out of the
visual reality around you.
Listen for sounds -- and sounds within sounds. Can
you hear the human cry?
Try new ways of smelling, tasting, feeling, moving.

EXPERIMENTING with materials
Spread out many different kinds of art materials
and tools. Try materials you've never used before.
See what each can do. Don't worry about what it
might look like. Let the materials "play" in the
fullest sense of the word. Combine two or three
kinds of materials.

CENTERING DOWN

FOCUSING on a special problem
PLANNING
CHOOSING

After an opportunity for free and spontaneous experimenting, the people will feel a need for CENTERING DOWN on a particular creative problem. The choice often develops from the beginning experience. TIME and CONCENTRATION are necessary if the creating is to have some depth. You will notice that some people will prefer to work alone; others will still enjoy working in groups, but the groups will become more intense and thought-full.

A common problem in workshops is --
How to interweave people in creating:

We were working with forty-five people in a three-day workshop in Phoenix, Arizona. One idea for helping this group come together was the building of the frame weaving on the next page.

The frame was constructed with light, sturdy wood sticks about 7 feet by 3 feet. The dark red WARP (vertical threads) were fastened with a stapler. Small nails hammered a half inch apart work even better, but the work takes a little longer.

The people were invited to add to the weaving at any time during the weekend. Each person chose colors, yarns, found objects, or symbols that had personal meaning. The only directions given were to keep in mind the integrity of the individual work and the over-all inter-relating of the parts.

The weaving grew slowly during the three days. Many new things appeared after a TEXTURE WALK...a seeing-feeling exploration of the Arizona environment.

The closing celebration centered around the weaving. The people had created many things during the workshop: songs and slides, dance and drama. The weaving was a focusing on the possibilities of creating. In a way, it was still unfinished...waiting for more to be included. The weaving was a banner which told a history and at the same time, seemed to challenge further growth.

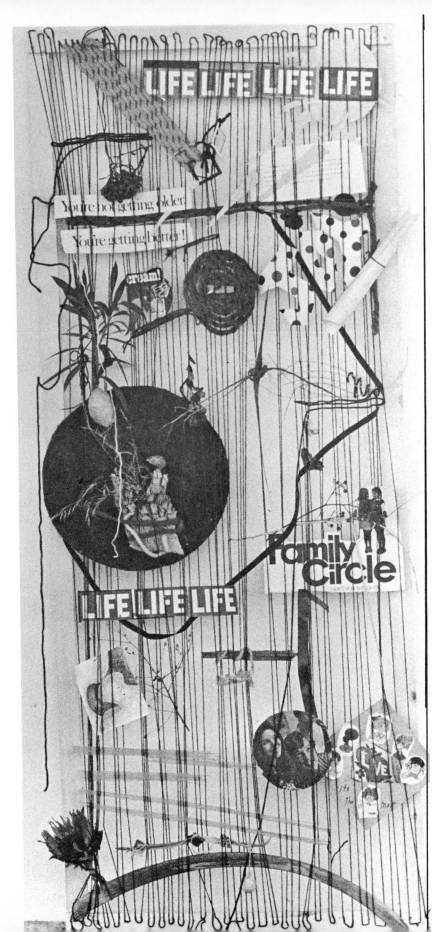

The key idea of
WEAVING PEOPLE
TOGETHER
THROUGH
EXPERIENCE
took a visual
form which
became a
memorable symbol.

11

BIRTHING

GIVING significant form

Birth is a slow process; yet all of a sudden it happens, and sometimes in unexpected ways. After much planning, designing, struggling, a whole new image may emerge which is far more significant than the first idea.

     In Boulder, Colorado, an ecumenical group of a hundred people were examining the meaning of THANKS-GIVING in contemporary life. An outcome of the work-shop was to be a Thanksgiving Celebration and banners that could be shared by the different churches in the Boulder area. The first "banner group" idea session resulted in nothing but cliché phrases and symbols. On the second evening of the workshop, everyone went out into the city to discover what would happen if they tried to give away five sticks of gum as gifts to any-one they might meet. The actual experience of having a gift refused, regarded with suspicion, laughed at, accepted with hesitation, or finally received and chewed, gave everyone fresh insight into <u>giving</u> and <u>receiving</u>. The image of the "gift-of-gum" became so important that one banner took the form of a huge gum wrapper with "THANKSLIVING" in place of "WRIGLEY'S SPEARMINT".

<u>CLUES</u> for <u>ENABLING</u> <u>SIGNIFICANT</u> <u>FORM</u>

Try not to rest with the first idea that comes along. It may be just a springboard for a better one. First ideas need refining. Probe a little more deeply into the meaning. Is this really a fresh statement?

A group might come up with several good ideas. By reshuffling and combining them, a much stronger expression can develop.

Sometimes the key to a more SIGNIFICANT FORM lies in simpli-fication. There is a tendency to try to put too much into one statement or design. Take away all the extras and let the main idea come through loud and clear.

If you notice a tension between wanting to get a project finished and yet not being satisfied with the way it is taking shape, it might be a good idea to get away from it for a while. Do something different. When you come back to it, you may be able to work out a whole new solution. One of the really important aspects of creativity is learning to find alternatives.

Another banner group had been attempting to express the community of concern that had been growing among the people from twenty-six different churches. The gum-experience had drawn divergent-thinking people into a close bond of friendship. The symbol of this unity had been drawn and cut-out in a complex, but strong arrangement of colors and line. The only difficulty was that there was no time to glue it all down on one backing. To solve the problem, the empty banner was brought in during the closing celebration. The pieces of felt were passed to everyone. Each person could add something to the pre-cut shape. All shared in putting the banner together. It was now, truly, a coming-together of each person in the group, especially when they all tried to glue things down at the same time. The final addition of the words: "COME UNITY" made the banner both a proclamation and a prayer.

SHARING

THE GIFT is offered and received

In the example above, the banner was creatively shared by everyone adding something to it. This is what happens in a real, but perhaps less literal sense, when a group responds to a newly created GIFT as the unique glimpse of reality that it is. Each reaction helps the individual artist gain a new understanding of what he has expressed. In order for this kind of SHARING to take place, it is necessary to set an environment that will help everyone feel at ease. A person needs encouragement when his first effort is out in public view. He feels exposed and vulnerable. He is often inclined to laugh at his attempt. The fact that a number of people take time to sense worth in his creation is tremendous support.

Some SHARINGS can be very simple, with a chance for everyone to really get inside what has happened in the process. The group should let the visual image speak for itself, first of all. What do the colors say?...the combinations of shape and texture?...the movement of lines? Usually the comments and reactions pick up different aspects of the work and provide further insight. Then the artist may be asked to trace the creative development of his work and add reactions of his own.

It is crucial for SHARING that each person has created something so that everyone knows the TENSION, EFFORT, and SURPRISE, that has gone into the making. When some people in a group do not create, they become spectators and critics rather than participators.

One Sharing Model:

   In a workshop, small groups of people made paper banners that said things like:

      "LIFE IS -- SHOUT IT!" with three-dimensional megaphones hanging at the bottom.

      "WONDER EXPLODES INTO LIFE!" with a circular explosion of color.

      "A DREAM TASTES BEAUTIFUL!" with dreams and hopes hanging as fruit on a real tree branch.

   We were seated in a large circle. The banners had the quality of surprise about them. They had been made in other rooms and were being seen by everyone for the first time. The group responded to the bright color and rich imagery with great enthusiasm. The designers were so pleased that their work actually communicated, that they were able to give a deep look into their own process of creating. This kind of SHARING is not likely to take place if the individual just starts out explaining how his work came to be.

   The banners were begging to be sung. First, we chanted the phrases in rhythms. Then we started making melodies. Because we were facing each other the sound had a stereo effect. Soon everyone was standing and moving to the rhythm. The sound grew spontaneously as descants were added. It ended with a loud, "LIFE IS -- SHOUT IT!"

Another Sharing Model:

Workshop groups in Toronto were sharing paintings of recent moments of meaning. One painting showed a dancing array of flowers against the texture of a cinder-block wall. As enabler, I asked the group to consider what the lines and colors said to them. "Joyousness"..."Growth"... "A buoyant spirit"...were some of the reactions. They were fascinated by the textured-wall effect. "It seems to contrast and yet support the freedom of the flowers," was one response. The designer explained that she had tried to paint what she felt while working with high school students. The bright flowers represented the enthusiasm and life that was there, despite all the criticism of formal structures. She had taped her paper to the wall. After painting for awhile, she noticed the texture from the wall coming through. At first it seemed to be a symbol of restriction. The group reactions brought out a new aspect -- structure as framework that could allow for and support freedom.

WORKING WITHIN GROUPS

I have frequently used the term group, referring to a small cluster of people who come together to share a creative experience. A group, however, is more than a cluster of people. When people get together there are different levels of meeting. There is friendly chatter, interesting conversation, discussion, argument, and so forth. This might be called association. It is not yet a group.

A COMMITTEE is not a group.
     A committee is usually appointed. It has an agenda.
     It has a chairman upon whom it depends for momentum.

A GROUP is an invitation to become person-al, to grow in a
                                             Spirit of freedom.
     It is made up of persons in relationship; people who can
     communicate face-to-face; who can be open to one
     another's views and experiences.

A CREATING GROUP is people who are willing to make a journey... discovering themselves...risking together...struggling for authentic expression and significant form...sharing a
                                   heightened awareness of life.
A CREATING GROUP is willing to search out the possibilities of communal celebration in a world that sometimes insists that there is nothing to celebrate.

HOW DOES A CREATING GROUP FUNCTION?

There is together-ness about a CREATING GROUP.
All participants share from the outset. Each tries to
understand what the others are saying.
There is no chairman -- no hidden agenda. The activity
and outcome will depend upon each person.

The group has come together for the purpose of finding
new modes of ex-pression. It is not turned in on itself,
but out from itself.
The inner growth which comes from creating together has
an outward thrust.

HOW CAN YOU ENABLE THE CREATIVE GROUP TO HAPPEN?

Make the purpose of the workshop or meeting very clear in
the information that is sent out or announced. People
should come knowing that they will be creating in a variety
of ways.

Offer the opportunity to as wide a range of people as possible. Groups mixed by age, by social, religious or professional backgrounds make the workshop more creatively
stimulating.

Flexibility of space should be considered in the planning.
There should be enough room for the entire group to be together and to divide into smaller groups for the various
activities. People should feel free to move around to
other groups if they wish, especially in longer workshops.
Try to allow for individual creating as well as group
activity.

Plan an opening DISCOVERING activity that will help everyone plunge in.

Let the people form their own small group clusters (5 to 8)
inviting them to join with others whom they've never met.

The first SHARING experience should happen in the small
group. It builds trust and genuine exchange of thought.
After the first sharing, the excitement and quality of
creativity rises. People begin to believe in themselves
and what they can do.

Part 2   THE VISUAL LANGUAGE

VISUAL LANGUAGE is non-verbal communication of ideas and
emotions. We use this language all the time. It consists of
such things as gestures, signs, facial expressions, or even
the clothes people wear. Pictures can tell a whole story.
Shapes and colors can evoke feeling. Simple lines can convey
a message.

The first step in understanding this expressive language is to
begin SEEING.

We SEE so much for granted.

              The whole world rushes in at us
                    an immense collage of images
                          screaming for attention.

We dim out as much as we can, in order to get on with the
business of the day. We need to take time to really LOOK.
Start with bright colors, shadows, patterns of dark and light.
What colors relax you? What shapes and patterns make you tense
or anxious? What kind of designs intrigue you?

You are probably much more aware of the visual design around
you than you think. Graphic artists work hard to achieve what
is called "stopping power", in order to gain attention.
You don't have to go to a flower show or an art exhibit. Just
start looking at the world around you. You'll see all kinds of
images visually speaking to you. Take time to sort them out.
Then, when you are ready to make a visual statement in fabric
or paint, you'll have a rich vocabulary from which to draw.

The pages that follow will point up various visual characteristics that will help sharpen your perceptions and help you to
SEE in new ways.

It takes something of a child-like openness to look at the
world with new eyes. It is not an ability you can learn so
much as a quality of being ready to receive the wonder and surprise of all that is around you.

This banner was designed for a conference on world poverty, economics and the arms race. I chose the images of buildings dwarfed by the nuclear cloud, a missile and a bare tree. The colors are shades of gray, black, white, with reds, oranges and golds outlining the cloud. The words at the bottom form a border pattern. They are purposely in low contrast to draw viewers more closely into the design before they read the words.

Let all creation
Praise the Lord!

The rhythms and lines, as well as the colors in this banner, sing of the energy and richness of creation. Words would be an intrusion.

Banners have the ability to alert people visually to what they can expect to experience in worship. They prepare us to hear God's Word and respond with song and prayer.

The colors are important communicators in this creation design. Imagine, if you will, bright yellow, pink and orange in the sun expanding to red and dark red colors above and shades of green and blue below. The design is worked in something of a mosaic style to add energy and flow. This kind of patterning needs to be done right with the material. Black yarn lines add touches of accent.

A banner of this kind can be used in many different situations. The center has a mandala effect. It lends itself to retreat environments as well as liturgies.

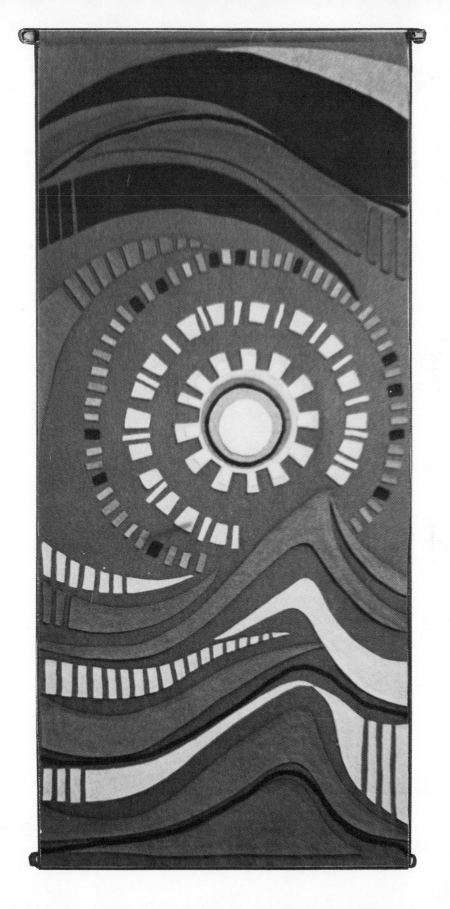

LINE

The VISUAL LANGUAGE is universal.
Through the ages the visual arts have embodied the history,
the beliefs, the very spirit of man. Art tells the story of
man's discovery of his world and his discovery of himself.

The basic elements of the VISUAL LANGUAGE are:

LINE   SHAPE   COLOR   TEXTURE

Putting these elements in motion adds another dimension.

By organizing and working with LINE, SHAPE, COLOR, and TEXTURE,
a person can create a visual representation of an event or an
experience. He can hand on to others feelings he has lived
through, so that they, too, can share in the experience. The
degree of sharing depends upon the ability of the artist to
authentically express his thoughts, and the sensitivity of the
viewer to receive it.

In order to master any language, it is necessary to understand
it and use it.

Let's start with *line*

A LINE seems like such a simple thing. It is nothing but a
point in space that begins to move, tracing its journey as it
goes along.

LINES can have lots of fun, and go where they want to go,

        or LINES can enclose space and represent things we
see in the world.

LINES are also expressive in the direction and combination
used. There is a natural sub-conscious impact to lines.
This expressive quality is due to the visual impressions we
have absorbed from our environment.

Here are a few basic line movements and some of the ideas
they communicate.

VERTICAL LINES

REACH UP.

They speak of GROWTH...PROGRESS...ESCALATION...POWER...STRENGTH...

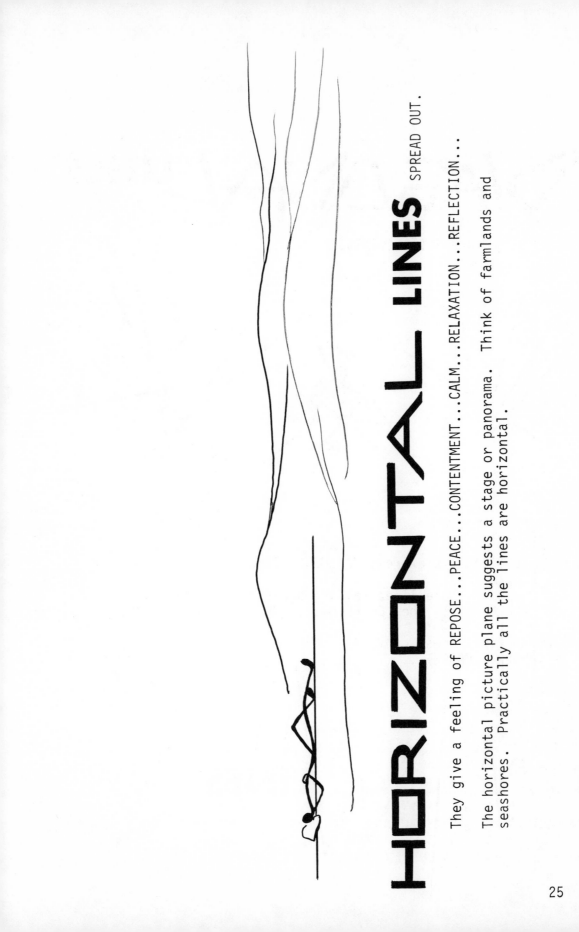

HORIZONTAL LINES SPREAD OUT.

They give a feeling of REPOSE...PEACE...CONTENTMENT...CALM...RELAXATION...REFLECTION...

The horizontal picture plane suggests a stage or panorama. Think of farmlands and seashores. Practically all the lines are horizontal.

25

DIAGONAL LINES

are ACTION LINES.

Simple diagonals express MOVEMENT...ENERGY...

More lines falling against each other
show CONFLICT...VIOLENCE...WAR...RAGE...

Jagged lines speak of
DANGER...FRIGHT...

EXPANDING LINES

SHOUT FOR ATTENTION!

Lines bursting out from a center speak of EXUBERANCE...
JOY...NEW BIRTH...SURPRISE...
You will find them in natural things like sunshine,
flowers, sprinklers, and jumping children.

Sein LINES

CURVED LINES flow and swirl. They may waltz around gracefully, meander lazily or tangle in confusion.

SPIRALLING LINES seem to grow with GENERATIVE LIFE.

When a LINE runs around and meets itself it becomes a SHAPE. CIRCLE shapes speak of WHOLENESS... COMPLETION... WELL-BEING... ABUNDANCE...

SHAPE

SHAPES exist all around us.
   TWO-dimensional shapes like postcards.
   THREE-dimensional shapes like houses and street lights.

A SHAPE is a solid mass. It has height and width.
   If it is three-dimensional, it has depth.

Usually we do not notice the general shape of a thing.
We see only its surface features. For instance, it's not
always easy to really see the SHAPE of a tree. The leaves
get in the way. Yet the leaves are a part of the shape.
It takes practice to be able to discern the real SHAPE of
things. Sometimes the shadow tells us more about the SHAPE
than the actual object does.

SHAPES can communicate in the same way that lines do.
When combined, shapes inter-act and set up certain movements
   within space.

Let's just look at some simple SHAPES:

   GEOMETRIC SHAPES...like building blocks, can be used in a
                never-ending variety of ways.

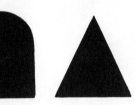

They are formed with compass and ruler and tend to express
      CONTROL...ORDER...LOGIC...

ORGANIC SHAPES are those we see in nature. They are growing shapes. They express life in its exuberant forms. This illustration is a photogram which gives us a chance to see the basic SHAPE clearly.

FREE-FORM SHAPES take on the freedom
    of the spontaneous.
They may lean toward the GEOMETRIC
    or the ORGANIC.

SHAPES may be POSITIVE or NEGATIVE.

POSITIVE SPACE is the SHAPE itself.

NEGATIVE SPACE is the empty area
    surrounded by the shape
 or the empty space around the shape.

In a design the NEGATIVE SPACE is
 just as important as the
                    POSITIVE SPACE.

This design incorporates both POSITIVE and NEGATIVE SPACE.

A small group made up of adults and teenagers had made non-verbal representations of their own particular world environment. It was the second session of a workshop. The people had come from different parts of Chicago and were quite interested in each other's backgrounds and outlooks. After the last person had shared his collage, Jean, a suburban housewife, said:

> *"Do you all see what I see?*
> *My world has everything in a careful, tidy arrangement.*
> *It's all centered around my own family and backyard.*
> *Look, Jim's and Tom's are the same way.*
> *Our pictures are all in boxes, while the young people*
> *have shapes and colors jumping around all over the*
> *place. Their world includes the whole of life."*

It was true. We all wondered why we hadn't noticed it. The striking contrast provoked new discussion. Jean added, "Why have I let my world and myself become so fenced in?"

In this instance, the SHAPES chosen, and the arrangement of them, told as much of the story as the actual pictures. Each person is unique in his particular choices and combinations of lines, shapes, colors, textures. We are all so influenced by our immediate environment that we need to expand our range of experiences in order to see what SHAPE we're in.

To experiment with SHAPES, cut out a variety of free-form or geometric shapes. Notice the interesting designs in the negative shapes usually thought of as scraps. See what you can make with them.

FRAGMENTING SHAPES

Take one of the positive SHAPES and cut it into pieces, keeping in mind something of the original shape. Paste it back together on a contrasting background, leaving spaces in between. Try to use all the pieces.

COLOR

sunlight → [prism diagram] → violet, blue, green, yellow, orange, red

COLOR speaks a very special language. It has a touch of
mystery about it. It is a gift of delight to the world.
Can you imagine a world of no color? Just shades of black,
white or gray?

COLOR gives the eye a grip on SHAPE. Colored objects seem
to be more familiar. COLOR tells us about the condition of
our environment. The diagram above shows sunlight passing
through a glass prism. The prism bends light and divides
the wavelengths which create color vibrations. All colors
are contained within white light. The sensation of COLOR
is crucial to our well-being. We are creatures of light.
Since it is the energy which furthers growth and expansion,
it has a quality of affirmation about it.

COLOR plays upon our IMAGINATION. It tends to be a bit
irrational. Colors evoke emotional responses, even if we
are not always conscious of them. Each hue exerts a particular effect upon us.

Close your eyes and imagine that you are walking into a room
painted bright red with touches of orange here and there.
How does it feel?

Now imagine walking into a pastel blue room with blue-green
decor. Does it feel any different from the red room?

There is a scientific reason for the psychological impact of
COLOR. Impressions received by the eye are instantly over-
laid by retinal memory of previous experiences, so that when
the eye sees red-orange, the mind usually adds ideas of fire,
heat, and whatever emotions these images suggest.

When the eye sees blue, the brain might add water, sky,
coolness. It's interesting to note also that colors toward
the red end of the spectrum require more tension on the part
of the eye muscles in focusing them than colors near the
blue-violet end.

COLORS near the red-orange end are called "hot colors"; and
those near the blue-violet end, "cold colors". Hot colors come
toward you, while cold colors recede.

COLORS involve other senses as well. We speak of loud colors
and quiet colors...soft colors...harsh colors...dancing colors.
We feel "in the pink" or perhaps it's "blue Monday".

Warmer and brighter colors tend to be joyful and exciting; darker,
colder colors are more inward and restful.

COLORS are hardly ever seen alone, and our perception of color
changes as different colors are placed next to each other.
An orange circle placed upon a background of yellow gives one
effect, while the same orange circle placed upon a background
of purple changes quite dramatically. You might like to test
this out with colors of paper or felt.

COLORS acquire meaning as they pass through a culture. Color
symbols of this type call forth an "intellectual response".
The institutions of church and government are most influential
in the development of color symbol. For example: the liturgical colors of the seasons, or the "red, white, and blue".
Think of the holiday colors, such as: red and green, orange and
black, red and white. Because of commercial over-use it is not
easy to make these colors mean anything else.

There's a magic in the mix of colors. Besides emotional and
symbolic color meaning, there is a distinctive quality about
color that sets it within a particular age or environment.

Prehistoric man was limited to the use of EARTH COLORS.
The colors of clay, charred wood, and various soft stones.
The Egyptians developed the beautiful deep turquoise blue.
The search for brilliant color continued as man experimented
with minerals and organic stains.

The Phoenicians worked with beautiful purples and reds.
In the Middle Ages things like egg yolk, wax, and resin were
used as binders, giving the pigment a special quality and
color tone. When oil painting techniques swept across the
Western world, a whole new era in art expression came into
being.

In our own age, the discovery of synthetic colors in plastic
and acrylic paints has added new colors to the scene. The
FLUORESCENT COLORS with or without black light create a
special atmosphere of excitement and vibration.

Each new type of paint or ink or dye has a characteristic
quality of its own, and asks to be handled differently. In
contemporary graphics and textiles we see examples of all
the types of color developed through the ages...EARTH
COLORS...EGYPTIAN BLUE...PHOENICIAN PURPLES...RENAISSANCE
REDS...as well as the HOT PINKS and SIGNAL REDS of today.
By using the colors of a certain era you can create an environment with historical or cultural overtones.

Artists become exceptionally sensitive to color. Most of
us use color intuitively. This often means the "trial and
error" method, and it works very well. If you want to find
out the effects of certain color combinations, the best way
is to make samples and try them out. There are so many
different shades and tints of colors in the diversity of
art materials available that you really have to see and experiment with the actual color samples. Become aware of
pleasing color combinations around you. Your eye for color
can be improved each day.

Some knowledge of COLOR THEORY will be helpful, though, in
planning color schemes. The COLOR WHEEL shown on the next
page is based on the sequence of colors in the spectrum and
shows color relationships. There are twelve basic COLORS
or HUES. It is the gradation and interweaving of related
hues that is the important factor in making colored surfaces
pleasing to our eyes.

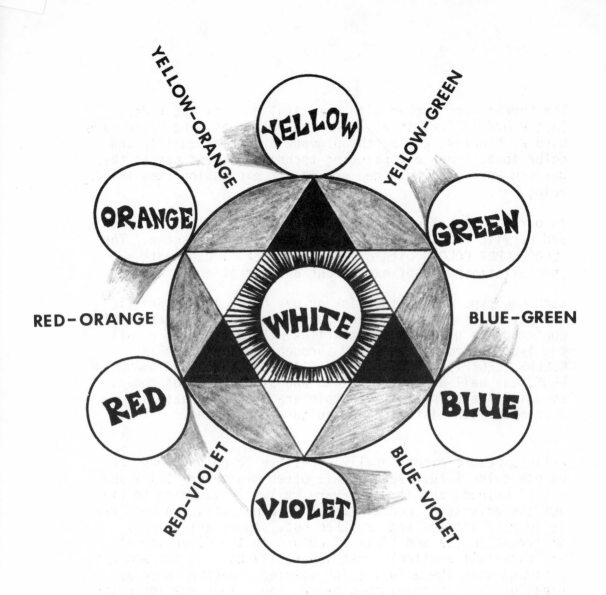

COMPLEMENTARY COLORS

Each color is closely related to another called its complement.
"COMPLEMENT" means that which completes a deficiency. In color
it is that which would need to be added to make white light.
COMPLEMENTARY COLORS are directly opposite each other on the
COLOR WHEEL.

COMPLEMENTARY COLORS are in direct contrast to each other.
When juxtaposed they create a strong optical vibration and
agitated movement. They "fight" each other. RED and GREEN
would be an example. However, shades of green with just a
touch of red for accent can create a pleasing effect.

COMPLEMENTARY COLORS occur in nature. Violet or blue-violet
flowers frequently have yellow centers. When you find a
butterfly with blue wings you will see flecks of orange in
the color arrangement. A red rose has bluish green stem and
leaves. The golden-orange sunset contrasts with blue-violet
clouds.

Here is an interesting experiment you might like to try:
    Take a sheet of brightly colored red paper. Stare at it
    without blinking for one minute. Close your eyes and then
    look at a piece of white paper. You will see the comple-
    ment of red. This can be done in the same way with all
    the other colors.

ANALOGOUS COLORS

Colors next to each other on the COLOR WHEEL are called
ANALOGOUS COLORS. They create a soothing, harmonious effect.
An example would be: blue, blue-green and green on the "cool"
side, and yellow, yellow-orange and orange on the "warm" side.

Wider skips on the COLOR WHEEL build color schemes with more
challenge. For instance: it's harder to balance orange, yellow and green.

Sometimes, when a color design does not seem to "hold together"
it will help to add varying tones of the same color or of an
analogous color. This might be called "echoing the color".
If a color arrangement seems harmonious but lacks vibrancy,
a touch of black or white may give it more life.

The language of COLOR speaks to each of us many times a day.
In spite of ourselves, we listen and react to it. COLOR is
something we can all use creatively and joyously to express
what we feel but cannot always put into words.

TEXTURE

Our world swims in TEXTURE. Everything has it.
We know TEXTURES through our sense of touch.
We SEE textures and know how they FEEL because we have felt
them before.
Imagine the feel of grass, fur, concrete.
Can you feel the grass without also imaging the LOOK of grass?

This inter-relationship between the visual and tactile senses
is referred to as inter-sensory blend.

Can you look at the picture of cactus on the next page without
sensing the prickles? Try to imagine the points as feeling
velvety to the touch.

When I showed the picture to a little seven-year-old and
asked her how it would feel, she said:

    "Ohhh! It would hurt! They must feel like needles."

She didn't know that the picture was a close-up of a large
cactus. In fact, she wasn't even sure just what a cactus was.
Her eyes told her that the pointed shapes were sharp and
painful.

TEXTURE communicates to us through sight and touch. It helps
us to understand the fabric of our world. Variations in surface texture seem to be necessary for our well-being. A
world of total sameness in texture would be unbearable. We
would not be able to exist. The astronauts on the moon spoke
of the disorientation caused by the moon's unchanging texture
of soft dust. A room devoid of all texture save the bare
walls becomes a torture chamber.

TEXTURE speaks of the actual condition of things. It invites
participation.

What is the TEXTURE of your environment? Try to collect some
samples of ordinary textural objects in your surroundings.
What do they tell you about life in your part of the planet
Earth? By becoming more aware of the TEXTURE of things a-
round us, we can become more "in touch" with existence. We
can also begin to understand the importance of TEXTURE in
visual designing.

Monoprint
by Hugh Wreisner

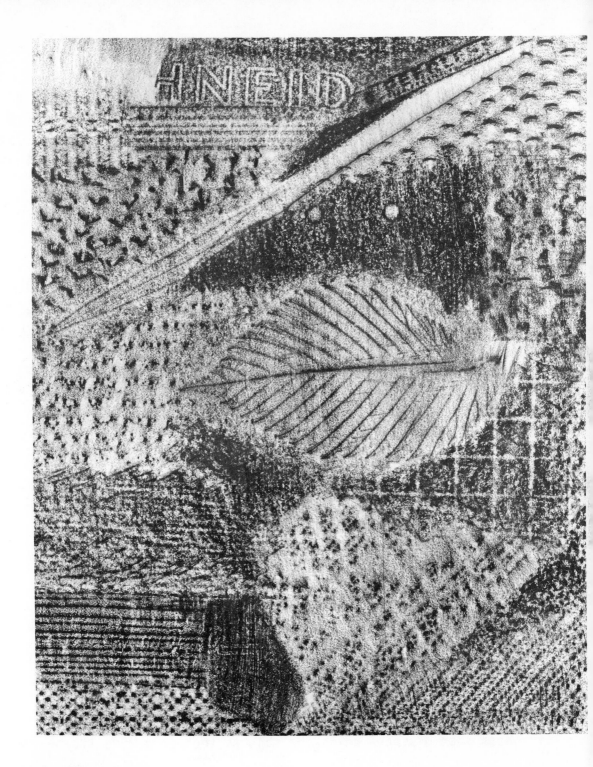

TEXTURE RUBBINGS

You can get a better understanding of TEXTURAL DESIGN by
collecting texture rubbings. All you will need is a black
crayon and some light weight white paper. Place the paper
on a surface and rub over it evenly with the crayon. Keep
the strokes in one direction. Look for textures with high
contrasts.

Another type of TEXTURE WALK that uncovers both sensitivity and imagination, is searching the outdoors for something that has a story to tell. A group at Loyola University explored the shores of Lake Michigan for objects that spoke to them. The search lasted about an hour. Some went off alone; some explored in groups of two or three. All took time to sense the environment in a new way.

The piece of driftwood and nail pictured here was one of the objects found. There was a certain shyness when the group re-assembled on the beach to share their stories. But the shyness soon disappeared as the objects took on personality.

The wood and the nail spoke of the pain that first brought them together...the service they performed through their strong bond...the many storms they withstood...the strange turn of events they witnessed...until finally they were broken from the pilings and cast up upon the sand to rest in the sun.

Found objects and textures can be incorporated into a three-dimensional panel of wood or some other solid backing.

TEXTURE PATTERNS can be pressed into clay. The example shown was fired in the Raku method and then mounted on wood. Seeds were used to complete the design. Epoxy is the most satisfactory glue for adhering hard surfaces.

Self-hardening clay is more practical for group experiences of this type. It dries to a stone-like hardeness without firing and can be easily painted or lacquered.

GROWING A **DESIGN**

A DESIGN really is something that grows. There is a certain
logic to it -- an ordering of parts, a balancing of shape
and movement. But it is also a lively, dynamic thing that
asks you to fill the empty space, resolve the hanging line,
or interrupted motion.

DESIGN cannot be taught. It is a perception which must develop within each person. It's one thing to look at a design
and say, "Yes, that is a fine composition." and quite another
thing to actually draw or arrange one. Begin with an experi-
mental attitude. Your first efforts may seem crude and
childish, but stay with it. The suggestions for creating designs that are given here will not mean very much until you
start trying them out yourself.

SOME ELEMENTS OF DESIGN:

      BALANCE - holds the design together
             may be symmetrical or asymmetrical
             requires imaginative manipulation of parts

      RHYTHM - depends upon repetition or interval
             creates a feeling of movement or flow

      STRONG CONTRAST - dark-light, large-small, etc.

      EMPHASIS - creates a focal point or center of interest
             something seems to grab your attention,
             pull you into the design

      VARIETY - a touch of spice...

      UNITY - lines, shapes, color, texture, movement,
            work together to form a pleasing harmony
            so that they seem to have grown that way
            together

A good DESIGN doesn't just happen, you have to work with it.
You may have to fracture, shift, re-align shapes. The hardest
part may be to simplify the design. Keep thinking, "Less
rather than more".

SYMMETRICAL DESIGN

Equal arrangement of Elements

Go on

ASYMMETRICAL DESIGN

The balance is FELT rather than arranged.

RHYTHM

You can sense a flow or beat.

Try growing some designs of your own. Use just black and white before you try color. PAPER WEAVING, as illustrated below, will help develop a strong sense of CONTRAST in size and shape as well as in dark-light patterns.

Start with a simple shape. Cut the WARP (vertical) lines into the paper. Do not cut completely through the paper. Leave a small, un-cut portion at one end. This will hold your strips together. Cut horizontal or WEFT strips with varying widths and shapes. Experiment for awhile before gluing. This type of designing can also be done with felt or other fabrics.

DESIGN is the expression of the individual -- his range and
       combination of experiences.

Look back at the DESIGN on Pages 20-21. This is an arrangement of positive and negative shapes inter-acting with each
other. Notice the different lines of movement pulling your
attention in different directions.

Where is the EMPHASIS -- the center of interest?

The large magenta and white shapes create the main structure
of the design. What is used to add VARIETY?

What kind of RHYTHM do you hear with this design?

What words come to mind?

Can you pinpoint an over-all feeling or idea that this inter-
pretation communicates to you?

Now experiment with some abstract shapes of your own. Watch
for interesting negative shapes as you move pieces around.
The use of overlapping forms and lines, rather than isolated
shapes, usually builds a more dynamic design. Shapes that
inter-weave tend to make a composition stronger. They help
develop the total rhythm of the surface.

Look at the world around you for design elements of REPETITION,
INTERFACE, GROWING PATTERN. DESIGN is the process of bringing
all these things into harmony. UNITY in design, as in life,
may be thought of as the compatibility of all the various parts.

LETTERING

LETTERING is a vital part of many banners. Whenever it is used it should be an integral part of the whole design.

It should, first of all, be LEGIBLE...

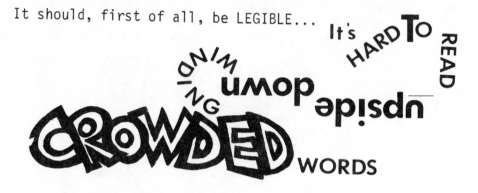

It should be compelling and pleasing to the eye. The style and placement of letters should harmonize with the rest of the design. The background color should be in strong contrast to the color of the letters.

LETTERING can make the difference between an ordinary and an exciting piece of work.

The type of LETTERING chosen should

COMMAND ATTENTION

EMPHASIZE MEANING

There is beauty in **STRAIGHT, SIMPLE** letter forms.

There is fun and playfulness in novel creations.

GOOD LETTERING requires patience, keen observance, great care and a touch of ingenuity.

50

The skill of SPACING is probably the trickiest to master. At first, it is a matter of trial and error. Spaces between words should be about the size of a full letter. Spaces between letters depends upon the letter shape. Shift the letters in words to equalize the area of white space between the letters.

Notice how the extra white space spoils the flow of the words.

This is an example of too little space between words, and an over-size letter.

These two words are hard to read because of poor spacing.

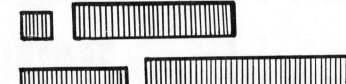

Plan your lettering layout in word blocks.

a PERSON
is an EVER-GROWING
network

abcde **ABCDE** abcd **ABab**

THE world Free of RUSH
SHOWN HERE needed now. Sight
DON'T you want, MORE

Study LETTER FORMS in magazines and newspapers.
Notice how different letter styles have
have different personalities.

ABCD AB ABCD
AB abc abcd
abc
ABCD AB ABC
abcde abcd abcd

52

Freehand LETTERING has a quality of uniqueness and
spontaneity about it. Try it.
You can draw or paint the letters...

Write with glue and cover it with yarn...

or you can tear the letters out in bold shapes.

Cutting Free-Hand Letters

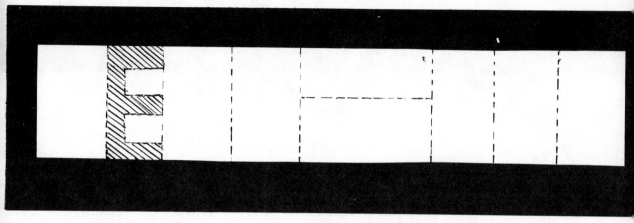

First, cut a strip of paper the height of the LETTERS
you want to make.

Try to visualize the LETTERS within the space.
Think of simple newspaper headline type.
Cut rectangles to correspond to the basic letter shapes.

ABCDEFGHIJKLMNOPQRST
UVWXYZ abcdefghijklmno
pqrstuvwxyz 1234567890

Here are some examples of more difficult letters:

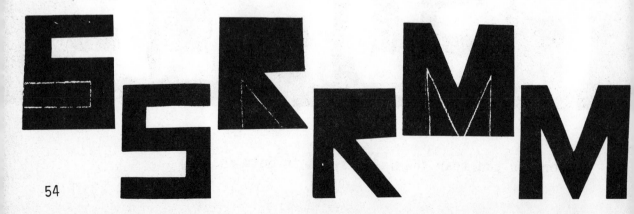

After cutting some of the plain box letters; begin shaping the letters in new ways. A little practice will give you more confidence. Your letters will take on personality. You will be able to develop your own distinctive style.

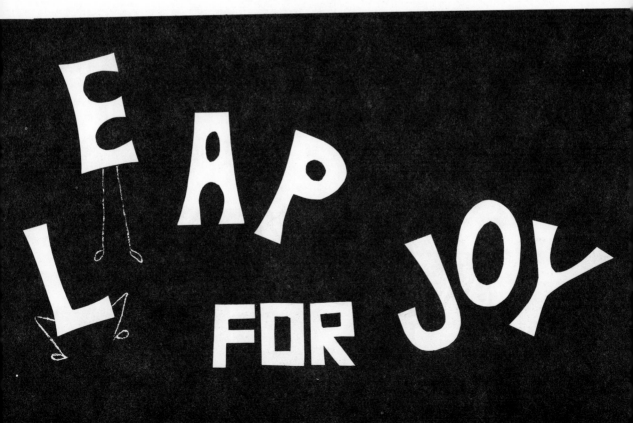

MAKE WORD **event**

Words have special energies, whether they are voiced or written. However, in a print-oriented, highly verbal culture the power of words has been imprisoned by saturation. We have lost the sense of the unique power of the word. In order to release this power, words need to be spoken and designed in fresh ways.

Selecting words which communicate the experience is part of the art of designing banners. Memorable phrases are more often the result of intense thought than of sudden inspiration. Do you remember the first words which Neil Armstrong spoke when he stepped onto the moon? His words had been carefully chosen for this history-shaping moment. They swept through time, linking past and future with the momentous now.

The words we choose for our banner should have the same quality of timelessness, having impact for the now, with an understanding of what has gone before and an anticipation of what is yet to come.

Words become EVENT-full when they express the innermost movings of God and man in such a way that the experience becomes available to me. The EVENT lives in me. It is not something a minister says to me or something I read in a book. Through the imagination of the banner's design the words become an immediate experience.

EVENT comes from two Latin words, *"e"* and *"venire"*, meaning *"out"* and *"to come"*. To make a word an EVENT means to let the full force of its meaning come out, to let it HAPPEN in a new way. A BANNER that is EVENT makes use of the visual power of the word. It creates a presence within space. It is not a decoration merely filling space. To shape words into EVENT may mean putting them together in striking contrast, or forming the letters of a single word so that they can awaken a new resonance.

The word WELCOME is used many times a day. What does it mean?
The design at the left is an expression of
child-like delight...
"It's fun to have you here!"

Part 3 NOW FOR BANNERS

WHAT IS A BANNER?

A BANNER is an EVENT celebrated in SHAPE, COLOR, TEXTURE,
and something MORE.

A BANNER can change an old, familiar environment into something fresh and alive, just by its presence.
BANNERS bring a NOW-ness into the group assembled at this
particular time. Like a newspaper headline, they can shout
out the heart of today's experience.

Since a BANNER doesn't just say a thing once...but keeps repeating it...whatever it says should have a newness about it.
Why keep saying things that have already been overworked?

BANNERS are not just contemporary decoration. They have a
quality all their own. They are different from flags or
protest signs. Aesthetically they certainly can be works of
art, but they are different from collages or hangings.

BANNERS and POSTERS are alike in some ways, but they are also
quite distinct in others. It is important to understand the
characteristics of each.

BANNERS and POSTERS:

> have a message to implant; an idea or thought to impart.

> should convey this message as clearly, concisely and
> effectively as possible.

> have a limited amount of space, therefore the design
> or illustration should be dynamic. Words should be
> kept to a minimum.

Distinctions:

a <u>POSTER</u>	a <u>BANNER</u>

basic purpose

a POSTER	a BANNER
Tries to sell something	States something I affirm
Is an advertisement or propaganda	Is a center of meditation
Must catch the eye and communicate instantly	May be a risk
Tries to motivate to a later action	Is poetic rather than didactic

style

a POSTER	a BANNER
Mass-produced	Made individually
Printed on slick-surfaced papers	Usually one-of-a-kind
	Textured -- has the feel of daily life
Disposable	Made of more durable materials
	Re-usable
Holds up super-idols of today -- personality cult	Proclaims a fresh-sensing of a shared belief
Multi-million dollar business	Contribution of personal time and talent

<u>POSTERS</u> are extensions of people -- of our culture.

<u>BANNERS</u> are extensions of people -- of our hopes.

BANNERS are a lifting up of sincere feeling. This can be done with words, or abstract shapes and colors, or with symbols that have real meaning for the people involved.

BANNERS SHOULD SOMEHOW INVITE PARTICIPATION

      THEY SHOULD REACH OUT AND TOUCH THE HEART.

They can be made from an endless variety of materials and hung in all sorts of places, but there are three ingredients every banner should have:
    a bright splash of color
        a song to sing
            and someone who cares.

The first step in the process of actually making BANNERS is

COLLECTING THE MATERIALS

The materials used in banner-making should have a wide variety
of TEXTURES. They are part of the fun that comes with making
the banner. Interesting materials spark a desire to create.
Be a good scrounger.

Materials:

felt	shells
burlap	driftwood
canvas	sand dollars
drapery	bells
vinyl plastic	prickly weeds
velvet	hemp (sisal)
satin	slender branches or twigs
novelty woven textiles	copper screening
upholstery fabrics	beads
yarns, threads, cords	leather
rick-rack	plastic or wooden rings
nets	

FELT is the most commonly used fabric for banners. The colors
are gay and vibrant. It is easy to cut and the edges do not fray.
It can be glued or sewn. It hang well. It is expensive to use
for the background material, but is within most budgets if used
for letters and designs.

BURLAP makes a good background. It is inexpensive and has an
interesting texture. The edges can be fringed and knotted.
Large letters can be made with burlap. Catch or seal the frayed
edges on the reverse side with a bit of glue before applying to
the background. The only drawback with burlap is the fact that
it fades easily.

Some drapery materials have hand-woven textures and are fade
proof.

The use of clear plastic vinyl for a background gives the banner
a very contemporary look. It is necessary to hand-sew the
pieces of felt or fabric to the plastic material. Glue will not
hold.

SEARCHING OUT MEANING

After a group has had a chance to <u>see</u> and <u>feel</u> the materials they will be using, it is time to begin the search for a significant expression in word or symbol.

BANNERS IN GROUPS

BANNERS are not just something added-on to brighten up a celebration. They should lift up a key image or phrase. It is all too easy to fall back on quotes from books or posters; to repeat trite phrases, cultural cliches. It's hard to make words like PEACE...JOY...LOVE...sparkle with newness. The problem is to find new expressions, new statements, new rally cries. It's unfortunate, but true, that most really important cries do not get into churches until two years later. By this time they have become policy or have been commercialized to death. The whole Peace Movement is a glaring example of this. Before long we'll probably have Superstar banners decorating the church. Christian artists should be at the cutting edge rather than in the second-hand shops.

The BANNER-MAKING group, when it is part of a larger group developing a particular celebration, should have a clear grasp of the movement or journey the celebration will be taking. They should keep in close touch with the rest of the planning groups. If the banner or banners are to be an integral part of the action, they must grow as the celebration grows.

Besides keeping in touch, the BANNER-MAKING group should be involved in all the experiences that will lead to the designing of the celebration. They should keep their ears tuned for significant phrases and expressions used by people as they brainstorm for ideas.

In a workshop at Heidelberg College in Tiffin, Ohio, fourteen long banners were made in a few short hours, on brown paper with paint, felt markers and collage material. The banners filled the room with a new sensing of man and hope for the future. The designers had been part of the group of students trying to understand man's relationship to a technological world. They had been discussing the value of an individual person. From the thoughts that emerged they devised a survey question to discover how their fellow students valued a person. The question was: HOW DO YOU RATE A PERSON'S WORTH ON A SCALE FROM 1 TO 10?

It was a hard question to answer and a harder one to ig-
nore. When the students returned to share their findings
they were surprised...impressed...and finally elated to
learn that people placed a much higher value on the indivi-
dual person than they would have guessed. The students also
found themselves becoming involved in some penetrating dis-
cussions with unlikely people. This was the kind of imput
that brought forth a wealth of expressive statements.

The fourteen banners served a dual purpose. They helped
cover windows in the student lounge to block out the light,
thus creating the necessary darkness for the multi-media
sections of the celebration. And they changed the familiar
lounge into a place with something to say.

INDIVIDUAL BANNERS

Sometimes there is a need for an INDIVIDUAL BANNER that is not
part of a Celebration, It is still just as necessary to search
for a significant phrase. Some groups can be triggered by a
single thought-provoking question like:

WHAT WOULD YOU REALLY LIKE TO SAY TO PEOPLE IF YOU HAD
            JUST ONE MORE CHANCE TO SPEAK?

The banner at the right was designed in response to the questions:

WHAT WOULD YOU LIKE TO TAKE BACK TO YOUR PEOPLE?
WHAT WOULD YOU LIKE TO SAY TO THEM?

Reverend Gary Bruening and his wife are from Minnesota.
They were attending our workshop in Denver, Colorado, that
city with the amazing backdrop of the Rocky Mountains.
They had once lived near the mountains and had grown to
love them. They wanted to bring back something of that
uplift of spirit that the mountains evoke. The words came
slowly. Gary had never made a banner. He struggled with
materials and ideas until finally the right words and de-
sign took shape. It was a simple statement. For him, the
mountains said it all. But would the people back home
understand? He began to expand his idea and gradually the
lyrics for the song on the next page came into being. His
wife composed the melody.

BANNER by
Gary Bruening

HOPE IS LIKE A MOUNTAIN

GARY BRUENING   CARLYN BRUENING

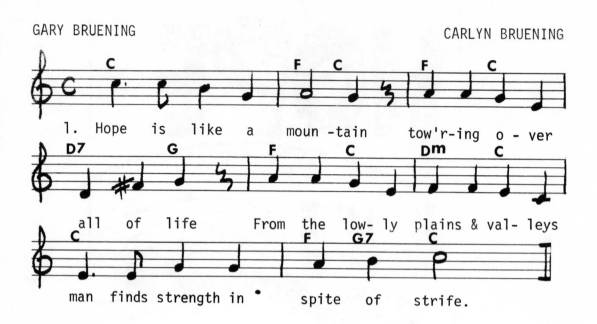

1. Hope is like a mountain tow'r-ing o-ver all of life From the low-ly plains & val-leys man finds strength in spite of strife.

2.   Hope is like a mountain
     Looking up from far below
     Man seeks meaning in existence
     And a faith to help him grow.

3.   Hope is like a mountain
     Not always easy to achieve
     As the pathway rises steeply
     Man cries out in disbelief.

4.   Hope is like a mountain
     Always there to draw man higher
     Don't give up, just keep on climbing
     Toward the victory you aspire.

This is a good example of the use of symbol and word. For Gary the mountains symbolized HOPE and MAN'S SEARCH FOR MEANING, but the symbol needed amplification so that others could share in the significance.

When, last week did you feel most like a HUMAN BEING?

THE HUMAN INSTANT

Another way to SEARCH OUT MEANING is to approach it in a non-verbal way. To help people begin probing their own experiences, ask them to think about the past week and recall an incident where they felt or realized what it meant to be human. In other words, they should try to remember an instant that gave them a glimpse of light about themselves or another person.

Have art materials handy: colored cardboard, scissors, glue, yarn, wire, magazines, markers, etc. Ask the people to express the incident in a non-verbal combination of the various art materials. Allow about 15 to 20 minutes for the work and then ask them to form clusters of 4 or 5 people (preferably people whom they do not know) and share the visual constructions. The people will discover that in sharing the symbol it takes on new meaning and depth. It is enriched because it is celebrated.

SYMBOLS are attempts by man to wrest meaning from his daily experience of life -- meanings which might be able to transcend and explain life. A SYMBOL points, not to itself, but to something beyond itself. From its Greek roots it means "to throw together"--"to compare". By creating new symbols out of our own sensings of life we throw together the dichotomies and tensions in order to deal with them.

When sufficient time has been given for sharing the symbols, gather the people into one group again and ask them to write a short phrase that crystallizes the experience for them. This phrase, along with the visual symbol, may well be the basis for a genuinely forceful banner.

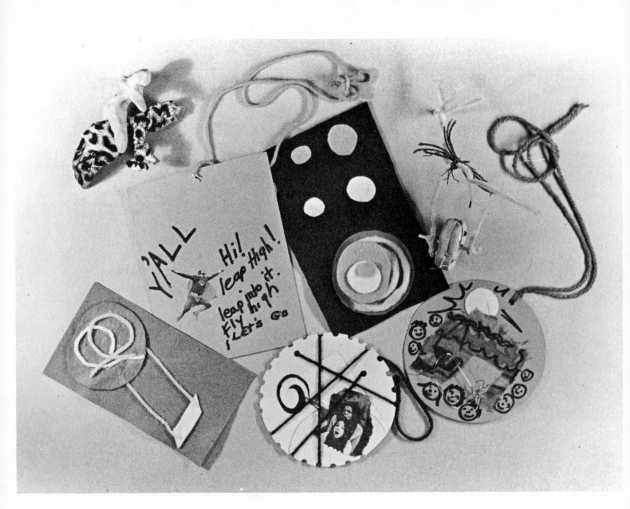

Here is a collection of non-verbal expressions from various workshops. They are sometimes used in place of name tags. They say much more about a person than the "HELLO! MY NAME IS" type. Each of the examples has a story to tell and symbolizes a very special human instant.

The swing hanging down from the bright orange sun conveys a feeling of "up" in a way that words could never quite match. The Superman figure was all alone in his leap through space until he was passed around the group and each person added a word or two. The clay man riding a tiger in the upper left-hand corner, speaks of one person's attempts to weather the "present shocks" of a changing world. The dark rectangle in the center pictures four members of a family as four separate islands. During the previous week the man had taken time to listen and talk with his older son late into the night. It was a break-through that seemed to re-establish the family circle of mutual interest and sharing. The strange little pipe cleaner figure with a wheel is a happy non-conformist on a unicycle, peddling his own way through a speeding, four-wheeled world. The last two are contrasting worlds. What do the lines, shapes and faces say to you?

A group might be interested in SEARCHING FOR NEW MEANING in Scripture. Ask them to take a Scriptural phrase (which is our heritage from the past) and bounce it off cultural phrases of our present day. This might provide the inspiration for a fresh visual treatment that could bring new meaning to both. An example would be the phrase:

YOU ONLY GO AROUND ONCE IN LIFE...

A BANNER is closer to poetry than to prose. HAIKU, a short Japanese verse-form, may be of help to a group searching for meaning. A HAIKU consists of three non-rhyming lines of seventeen syllables. The first and third lines contain five syllables, the second line contains seven. In the Japanese form there is always some reference to nature. The season is inferred by some key word. There is also usually an implied identity between two things which are seemingly different. The last line contains a "surprise" or a lifting up of the observation noted in the first two lines. The HAIKU does not always make a clear or complete statement. The reader is asked to add his own imagining and remembering to the poem.

HAIKU is an enjoyable form to use for your own creating. The discipline of the seventeen syllables helps you to discover the essence of your thought. The lack of rhyme allows for a freer expression. The use of metaphor encourages a playful yet meditative style. The exact HAIKU form need not be rigidly enforced. Some people may prefer to write free-form verse of their own. The HAIKU can be a jumping-off-spot for stimulating poetic sensitivity.

Here is a HAIKU that captures the imagery of the BANNER on page 69:

>
> SEEDS GROW TO SON'S WARMTH
> STRUGGLE UPWARD...ROOTS DRIVE DEEP
> GIVE US COURAGE TO TRY

PUTTING IT ALL TOGETHER

The making of the BANNER can be CELEBRATION.
Once the group has decided upon what it would like to say, some
organization is necessary to get the banner started. Usually it
is a good idea to make a sketch to get a picture of the general
lay-out. Individuals can choose to create the various words or
symbols needed. The banner at the right was made in this way.
The different styles in lettering add strength and variety, yet
they all work together. It is important at this point to recall the elements of VISUAL LANGUAGE that are developed in the
first part of the book.

Note especially the outline used with the white letters. White
letters alone on a yellow background would practically disappear.
It was crucial for this banner to be legible from the back of
the church. It was a litany response for a Lenten Celebration.
Each person in the congregation held a seed as the meditation
began:

> Lord, we are present here before you -- like seeds,
> encased in hard shells. Why have we allowed ourselves
> to be sealed in by walls of mistrust or apathy or whatever?
> Give us the strength to want to break out!
>
> *LORD, HELP US TO GROW!
> GIVE US THE COURAGE TO TRY!
>
> Let the real impact of your PRESENCE, the warmth of your
> CARE shine on us and draw us into the light!
>
> *
>
> Let the moisture of human needs seep beneath our shells
> and quicken the life energy within us.
>
> *
>
> The first new shoot piercing through hard, sometimes
> frozen soil, is terribly delicate and vulnerable.
>
> *
>
> But once the light is reached, the seedling begins to
> gather strength and green hope.
>
> *

IMPROVING THE DESIGN

As the banner progresses, lay out the main shapes, lines, words. Even though the preliminary sketch may have been carefully designed, changes often need to be made when the design is translated into fabric. Leave extra room at the bottom. The banner will be seen hanging. Shapes tend to become heavy. Sometimes a good banner is spoiled by the letters which seem to fall off the bottom.

Before the gluing starts, view the whole lay-out from a distance. Ask yourself:

>*Does the design fit the space?*
>*Are the colors and textures repeated to make a*
>   *pleasing unity?*
>*Are there any dingy colors?*
>*Is there enough contrast?*
>*Are the words legible?*
>*Is the banner cluttered?*

This is the time to be critical, not after it's all finished.

EXAMPLE:

LORD looks like a very strange word spread out this way. COME TO US is falling off the banner. The candle looks as if it were sweating.

LORD is rearranged and overlapped. The candle is simplified. COME has been re-cut to pick up the sweeping lines of the light rays. TO US has been eliminated.

before   **after**

If the banner is being made by a group, the whole process of refining the design will require much give and take. No one likes to see his own particular part eliminated. Even when an individual is working alone, it is hard to take out parts that have required a lot of work but really do not fit with the rest of the design. Sometimes these parts can be used in other banners. The important thing is that people understand why the change was made.

The easiest and quickest way to assemble a banner is to use a white glue that will dry clear. Usually a line of glue about 1/2 to 1/4 inch in from the edge will secure the piece. Keep in mind the fact that the banner will be hanging. Large areas or pieces of fabric will need to be covered with a series of glue lines so that they will not sag when the banner is hung. The gluing should be done as carefully as possible. Glue spots can be removed with a damp cloth if they are taken care of before the glue dries completely.

The large areas should be glued first, then the smaller shapes. If yarn letters or details are a part of the design, they should be done last. Let the banner dry thoroughly in a flat, spread out position. You might even want to weight some areas.

Banners also may be sewn together by machine or by handwork. This gives a more permanent quality to the material. The machine stitch, especially the zig-zag, can add fascinating line work. Very large banners may need to be sewn in order to hang well. Hems, especially at the top, are usually put in by machine stitch. The top hem should be wide enough for a dowel rod or a 1 in. wide stick to be inserted easily.

VERY LARGE BANNERS

Design the banner carefully on paper. To enlarge the drawing use an opaque projector. Tape large pieces of paper (*the size desired for the finished banner*) to the wall. Move the projector until the image is the size wanted.

or

Design the banner on graph paper. Make graph lines on your large pattern paper. A 1/4 inch square, for instance, might represent a 10 inch square on the enlarged scale drawing.

STITCHERY and APPLIQUE'

Embroidery stitches and applique' techniques can be used to great advantage in finishing a banner. It is possible to be a painter in thread. The stitches can be made with heavy yarns, metallic threads, embroidery floss, etc. Large areas can be sewn by machine with extra touches added by hand. Buttons, beads and other light objects can be sewn into the design.

FOR A THREE-DIMENSIONAL EFFECT try padding the applique' pieces with cotton before sewing. An even easier way, is to sew the pieces to the backing by machine, make a slit in the back and stuff the section to the desired puffiness. The slit in the back can then be closed with an overcast stitch.

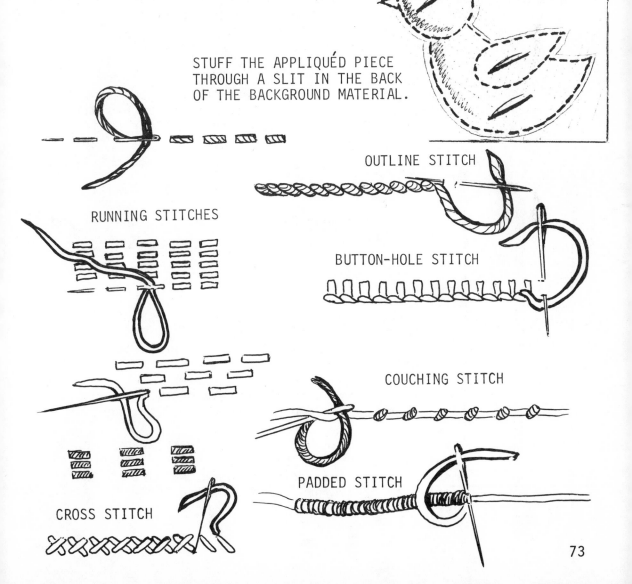

STUFF THE APPLIQUÉD PIECE
THROUGH A SLIT IN THE BACK
OF THE BACKGROUND MATERIAL.

RUNNING STITCHES

OUTLINE STITCH

BUTTON-HOLE STITCH

COUCHING STITCH

CROSS STITCH

PADDED STITCH

73

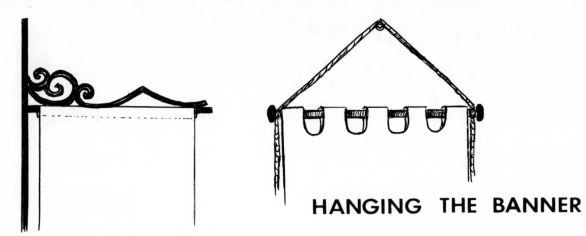

HANGING THE BANNER

Give adequate attention to the mounting and hanging of the BANNER. Your craftsmanship will be very evident and will either add to or detract from the over-all effect.

All BANNERS require some kind of supporting rod through the top seam. The BANNER will hang much better with a similar rod in a seam at the bottom hem. This is not always necessary. It will depend upon the weight of the BANNER. Curtain weights can be used as an alternative.

BANNERS made with light material will need to be lined. There are many types of drapery lining available. Felt banners will not need lining. It is possible to use both sides for design-work.

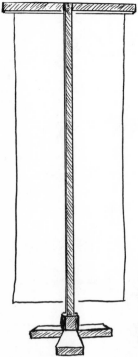

BANNERS can be hung flat against the wall.

Two-sided BANNERS can be hung from the ceiling or a beam.

Swinging wall brackets will hold the BANNERS out from the wall.

BANNERS can be supported by free-standing holders. This type allows for the most flexibility. The BANNERS can be carried in and easily arranged in the holders.

Various types of changeable display framework might be devised to meet particular needs.

Along with the BANNERS, you may want to make a matching cover for the altar (antependium) or a covering for the lectern. You might even be interested in designing a co-ordinating stole or vestment for the celebrant.

74

BANNERS IN CELEBRATION

The role of BANNERS in CELEBRATION can take many forms. One minister put the BANNER in the pulpit area and let it be a five minute sermon. It caused more comment than most sermons.

A priest in a small country church in Arizona designed a translucent curtain for behind the altar space in the sanctuary. Colored lights projected from the back, silhouette any shapes or letters applied to the curtain. Each week a different family has the opportunity to create a banner design for the curtain. Paper or cardboard pinned to the back of the curtain can be as effective as rich fabric when the lights provide the color.

Textured BANNERS can be hung in accessible places so that people can feel as well as see them.

For a special Celebration, the University Church of the Disciples in Chicago, found an unusual way to make BANNERS an immediate experience for the people. Three-foot wooden sticks with cross-bars were taped to each row of pews in the church. As the people entered, they were greeted by tables of banner-making materials and invited to make a BANNER for their section. The work was simple and fun. Instead of just sitting and waiting for things to start, the people found themselves caught up in the festivity of the occasion. They shared the making with family, friends and strangers alike. Pins were used as well as glue. The BANNERS were a special kind of offering and at the end were carried down the aisle and out into the neighborhood in a joyous procession.

The use of BANNERS is unlimited. Your ingenuity will suggest all sorts of alternatives once you get started. BANNERS can help an old familiar environment become fresh and new for this day...but not if they stay up to collect two years' dust. If BANNERS become permanent, like wallpaper, their charm is spoiled and their impact weakened.

Part 4   AND SUCH

This section presents a collection of ideas and techniques for
the making of many different things which can help create an
environment for celebration. Some of the ideas can be worked
into banners. Some are used along with banners to make a
gathering of people come alive.

BATIK is the first technique described. The people at Wheadon
Church in Evanston, Illinois, made a CRAYON BATIK hanging for
Easter. It extended from the ceiling to the floor on the wall
behind the altar.

The work was begun six weeks before Easter. Anyone interested
was invited to stay after the Sunday services and help with
the project. The response was enthusiastic, drawing young and
old together in the absorbing work of designing and painting
colored wax on the fabric.

The design began with a tall, graceful Tree of Life. Birds
and flowers came to live in the tree. Human figures with up-
lifted arms joined in the Hymn of Praise. The finished product
was not only a work of art, but a real EVENT. The colors, the
joyous flowers and birds, the up-reaching lines, sang of rebirth
and Easter gladness. The BATIK was a visible sign of people
working together. Although there were no words on the hanging,
it was a constant reminder to the people of that congregation
that they have much to share with each other.

The BATIK process is a wax-resist method of
dyeing fabric. It is an ancient art which
originated in Southeast Asia. Banners and
hangings made in this manner take time and
artistry, but they are especially beautiful.

This illustration is a close-up study of a
BATIK hanging. The crackled effect is a
distinctive mark of the BATIK method.

BATIK

MATERIALS needed:

Suitable fabric (cotton, silk, or linen)
Wooden frame
Tacks
Brushes (small, medium and wide)
Bees wax and paraffin
Can and double boiler for melting wax
Electric hot plate or stove
Large, wide-mouthed jars or containers
        suitable for submerging fabric
Dyes (regular fabric dyes, liquid or powdered)
Fan (helpful in speeding up the drying process)
Newspapers
Paper toweling
Electric iron
Rubber or plastic gloves

Since BATIK is a process that goes from a light color to a dark
color, the material used must be light in color or white.
Natural fiber fabric should be used. The synthetic materials do
not retain the dye color. China silk and light weight cottons
are particularly desirable because the wax penetrates easily
and the colors take well. Wash the cloth in mild soap and
rinse thoroughly. When it is dry stretch the material, not too
tightly, on a wooden frame.

Next, melt some bees wax mixed with paraffin in a small can.
It's a good idea to use the double-boiler method for heating
the wax. A small electric hot plate will keep the water and the
wax hot. Try to keep the heat constant. The wax must be hot
enough to penetrate the material.

Dip a brush in the wax and draw your design on the fabric.
After blocking out all the portions of the design not to be
dyed, remove the fabric from the frame and dip it in a large
jar of light colored dye. The dye will color all but the
waxed parts of the fabric. Use gloves to protect your hands
when handling dyes. The dye is not harmful but it will stain.

With the first wax on the material, re-stretch it on the frame. Allow the material to dry thoroughly and then continue to add wax to the design. Remove the fabric again and dip it into a slightly darker color of dye. This process may be repeated until the desired number of colors from the lightest to the darkest have been used.

Before the last dye bath, if the crackled effect is desired, crumple the material into a tight ball and swish it around in the dye. The color will penetrate into the crinkles.

When the material is dry it should be ironed between pieces of newspaper or paper toweling. Keep replacing the saturated with fresh layers. Complete elimination of wax is obtained by submerging the material in oleum or turpentine.

CRAYONS ON CLOTH

Very beautiful and unusual banners can be made by using crayon on almost any kind of white or light-colored fabric. The easiest way to do this is to tack the cloth down on a smooth surface so that it is tightly stretched, with the threads running straight up and down and across. Plan your design for large, bold effects. Sketch or trace the outlines of it on the cloth. Press very heavily with the crayon. Make your strokes go up and down, and then across, when filling in the solid areas of color, so that the weave of the material will be filled with wax.

When all the colors have been worked in, put the cloth between two pieces of shelf paper or drawing paper, with the crayon side facing down. (Do not use newspaper. The black print sometimes transfers into the design.) Take a warm iron and carefully move it over the paper, trying to cover the whole surface evenly. Don't leave the iron in one spot too long. The warm iron will melt the crayon wax into the cloth making a permanent design. The cloth can even be washed if you handle it gently in mild soap.

CRAYON BATIK

This method is sometimes called "INSTANT BATIK". It's not quite "instant" but it is less complicated and a little faster than the traditional technique. The colors of CRAYON BATIK have a unique character. They are brilliant and translucent.

MATERIALS needed:

    Wax crayons
    Paraffin
    Cotton fabric
    Fabric dye
    Brush (1/2 in. wide)
    Muffin pan and baking pan
    Small hot plate
    Newspapers
    Paper toweling
    Iron

Sketch your design on the fabric. Decide upon your colors. Peel the crayons and break them into the individual muffin tin cups; 1 color (3 or 4 crayons) per cup. Drop a 1/2 in. cube of paraffin in with each color. The paraffin thins the wax and helps it to penetrate the material. Use the bright colors of crayon. Dark colors will be lost.

Melt the wax by placing the muffin tin in a pan of boiling water. DO NOT PUT THE MUFFIN PAN OVER DIRECT HEAT.

Spread several thicknesses of newspaper over your working area. Place the cloth on top. Tape down the edges to keep the cloth stretched and even. Brush the melted crayon colors onto the cloth, leaving spaces between the colors. These spaces are important. They will dye a very dark color to set off the bright colors of the design. The wax should soak completely through the material. If the cloth is too heavy for this, you will need to turn the cloth over and paint the design carefully on the back. Keep the wax heated and work rapidly trying to finish a color area before the wax dries. If the wax seems too thick, add more paraffin.

Melted crayon-wax is
painted into the design.
White areas are left
untouched by the wax.

The cloth has been dyed
in a dark color. The wax
has been ironed out. The'
The color remains, plus
the crackle effect from
the dye.

Let the wax dry thoroughly, then crumple the fabric gently into
a ball. The crumples in the wax surface catch the dye and make
the lovely "crackle" effect which is characteristic of BATIK.

Mix a strong solution of a dark-colored dye: black, brown, dark
green, purple, etc. Follow the directions on the package. Allow
the mixture to cool, then place the fabric in the dye bath for
about 10 minutes. Remove it from the dye and spread it out to
dry on newspapers or on the grass. Blot it with paper toweling.

To remove the wax, place the cloth between layers of paper
toweling and press with a moderately hot iron. The heat will
draw the wax from the cloth, leaving just the rich color. The
toweling will absorb the wax. You will have to replace the
paper several times, top and bottom. When no more wax comes
out, the BATIK is finished.

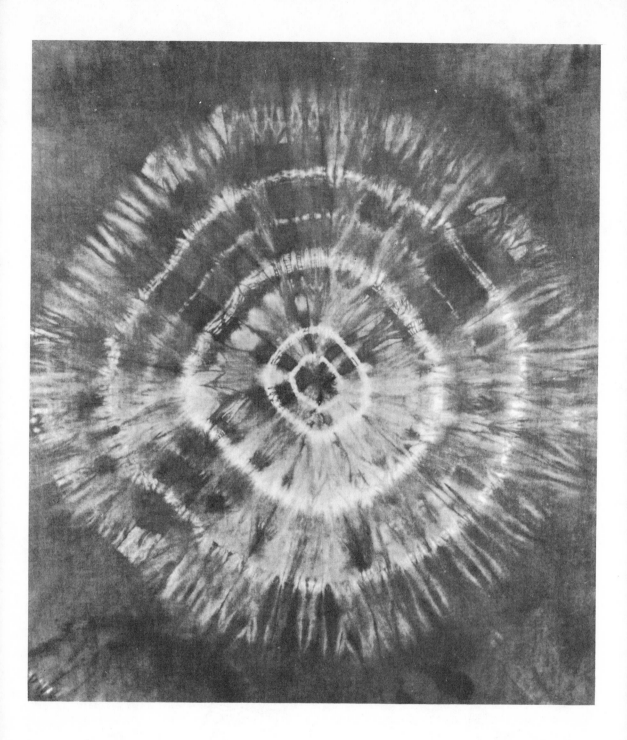

The radiant sunburst patterns of the TIE-DYE fabric make
unusual banners. Combined with BATIK or finished with a
BEAD or MACRAME fringe the TIE-DYE BANNERS can be stunning.

TIE-DYE

TIE-DYE is an easy way to add intriguing and vivid design to
fabrics. You will want to do much experimenting once you get
started.

MATERIALS needed: Natural fiber material
                          Fabric dyes
                          Large, wide-mouthed jars
                          String
                          Masking tape
                          Rubber or plastic gloves
                          Newspaper

The basic idea is to tie or knot the material so that some of
it will absorb the dye and some of it will not. You can tie
the whole piece of material in one big knot, or in several
smaller knots. You can tie off various sections of the cloth
with waxed string and rope. Different thicknesses of string
produce different effects. Masking tape wrapped around some
areas changes the pattern. You can fold, pleat, twist or
gather the material.

Cords can be dyed beforehand and not rinsed so that the dye color will bleed. Use sheet plastic for tying off wide areas. If the dye is to be completely resisted the area should be closely covered with wrapping.

Pebbles, seeds, plastic or glass objects, pieces of wood can be tied inside a tuft of fabric to create a variety of shapes.

Mix the dyes according to the directions on the package. The knotted and tied fabric can be dipped into one color entirely, or it can be dipped into a series of colors. Sharper, clearer resists usually result from dampening the tied piece before dipping it into the dyebath. Dye color can be poured over the knots. You can paint the dye into parts of the fabric.

TIE-DYEING and BATIK can be co-ordinated beautifully. The TIE-DYEING would be the first step, BATIK the second.

After dyeing the knotted fabric, let it rest for about 5 or 10 minutes to set the dye. Rinse if the directions call for it. Blot the fabric with paper towels. Untying is always left until the piece is at least semi-dry. Remove the strings and knots carefully. The dyed fabric should dry thoroughly. It is then ready for ironing and hemming.

TIE and BLEACH

Black or very dark materials can be used to make fascinating negative patterns. Tie or knot the material as you would for TIE-DYE and then put the whole piece or dip sections in bleach. You can watch the process. Take the material out when the degree of lightness desired is reached. Cold water will stop the bleaching. The material should be washed to remove all traces of bleach.

SPECIAL NOTES ON WAX and DYE TECHNIQUES

Try each technique yourself before you try it with a group.

Wax and paraffin are INFLAMMABLE. Great care and precaution should be taken in procedures for heating and handling the wax.

Plan to use work areas that will not be ruined by melted wax or splashes of dye. Some dyeing can be done outdoors.

Wear work clothes or a smock that covers well. Rubber gloves will prevent badly stained hands.

Cleaning-up will be simplified if work areas are well-covered with newspaper.

Any fabric to be dyed must be washed free of sizing with warm water and mild soap, thoroughly rinsed, and dried. Old sheets are good for experimenting, but will not always dye evenly.

Natural fiber materials rather than synthetic materials should be used in order to retain the dye colors. If you are not sure about a material make small sample tests before you begin.

Commercial dyes such as Rit or Putnam work satisfactorily. For best results follow the directions on the package. Professional dyes usually require boiling.

In designing the various kinds of cloth banners, allow plenty of room for hems. The selvedge can be utilized on the sides. The cloth should be hemmed evenly at top and bottom. Thin rods or doweling sticks inserted in the hems will enhance the banner and help it to hang well.

BATIK and TIE-DYE FABRIC can be washed in warm water and mild detergent. It should not be dry cleaned.

MACRAME'

MACRAME' is the craft of creative knotting. Like weaving, it appears to be quite complicated, but only two basic knots are involved -- the HALF KNOT and the HALF HITCH. These two knots can be used in an endless variety of ways to create the most exciting and intricate works of art.

MATERIALS needed: Scissors
                      "T" pins
                      Knotting board
                      Yarn or twine etc.

Yarns used for MACRAME' should be strong, smooth-surfaced, and should not have much give or elasticity. Heavy rope, twine and cord purchased in hardware stores can be used. Linen cable has strength, diversity of character and combines well with other yarns.

The KNOTTING BOARD should be made of material that is light-weight and rigid, yet soft enough for pins to be easily inserted. Celotex or corkboard make a good working surface. Sizes might range from 12" x 24" to 24" x 48". Cover the board with brown wrapping paper and mark it off into a grid of 1" squares.

DOUBLE HALF HITCH

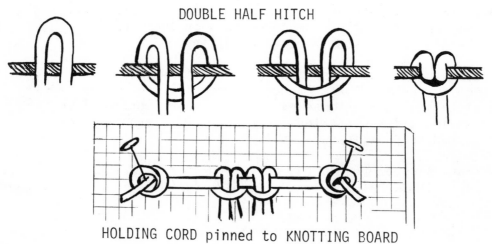

HOLDING CORD pinned to KNOTTING BOARD

TO BEGIN:
    Tie an OVERHAND KNOT at each end of the holding cord and pin them firmly to the KNOTTING BOARD. The cord must be kept taut. DOUBLE HALF HITCH knots are used to fasten the desired number of ends to the holding cord.

Half Knot

Square Knot
Continue
with
series of
Square Knots

Reversed Square Knot

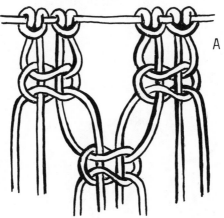

A KNOTTING PATTERN
for OPENWORK
SQUARE KNOT used
in alternating
rows

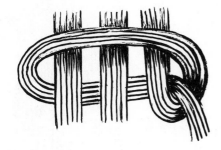

The Gathering Knot
This knot can be used to
make a knotted fringe
ending on burlap banners.

FRINGES

WAYS TO WORK BEADS INTO THE DESIGN

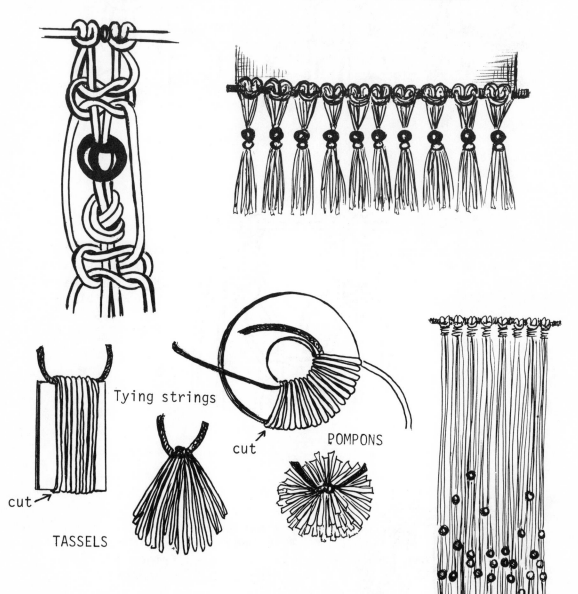

Tying strings

cut

POMPONS

cut

TASSELS

This is only an introduction to CREATIVE
KNOTTING -- just enough to get you started.
The knots shown here can be combined in
many different ways for fringes and design
work in banners. Found objects, bells,
beads and wooden rings can be used to great
advantage with MACRAMÉ.

WEAVING

WEAVING is an ancient yet ever new art that can be beautifully incorporated into BANNER-MAKING. Many people are fascinated by handweaving but hesitate to try it because it appears to be so complex. Looms may be of many types, ranging from very simple stick or frame arrangements to the large, complicated floor models with harnesses, treadles and so forth. But with all of them the weaving process is basically the same.

WEAVING is a process of interlacing threads at right angles to each other to form a web or fabric.

WARP is the arrangement of vertical threads that make the structural skeleton for weaving. The WARP threads are kept at an even tension.

WEFT refers to the horizontal fibers woven through the WARP. These are sometimes called the FILLING. The WEFT threads can be worked through the WARP by hand, or by a large needle or by shuttle.

Imaginative and highly artistic weaving can be done on very simple devices.

CARDBOARD LOOMS

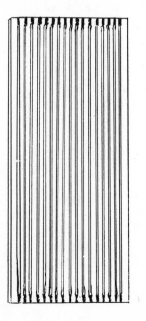 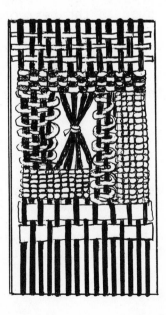 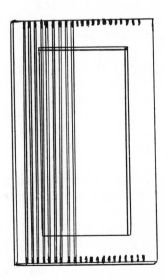

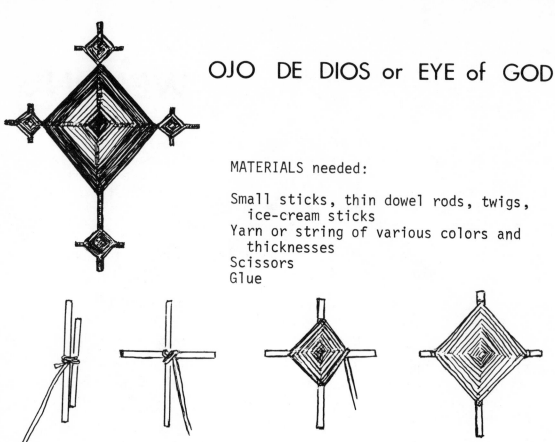

OJO DE DIOS or EYE of GOD

MATERIALS needed:

Small sticks, thin dowel rods, twigs,
    ice-cream sticks
Yarn or string of various colors and
    thicknesses
Scissors
Glue

Tie the two sticks together with the yarn you are going to use.

Open the sticks to form a cross. Begin wrapping the yarn a-
round each stick and then over to the next one, working out
from the center. To keep the wrapping in place, run a line of
white glue along each stick, a little at a time.

If you wish spaces between strands, wrap the yarn several
times around each stick, then go on to the next and continue
the pattern.

You can change the pattern by wrapping the yarn under and a-
round the stick instead of over and around the stick.

You can change color by cutting the yarn, tying in the new
color and wrapping the yarn over the knot to hide it.

The ends of the sticks can be wrapped with yarn. Pompoms or
tassels give a finishing touch, or you might want to add the
extra crosses on each end.

OJO DE DIOS or EYE OF GOD

This woven yarn cross is used by the Huichol Indians of
Mexico. The symbol actually pre-dates Christianity. The
"eye" is usually made with two crossed sticks. The traditional one consists of five "eyes" -- a center, large one made the
first year of a child's birth, and an additional smaller one
added on the ends each year until the child is five.

WOODEN FRAME LOOMS

Wooden frames are a versatile weaving loom. They can take any shape desired and lend themselves easily to innovation. The creative weaver will use imaginative approaches to design, avoiding monotonous strips of color and weave. Straw, weeds, fibers, nylon stockings, reeds, and yarns of every type can be combined with different pattern formations and open areas.

The Suspended Frame depends upon the heavy lower bar for the needed tension in the WARP.

Wooden frames or stretchers for oil painting can be made into looms. Simple frames can be constructed with soft wood and nails. TACKS, NAILS, or STAPLES can be used to hold the threads. The actual weaving can be done with the fingers or with very large wooden needles.

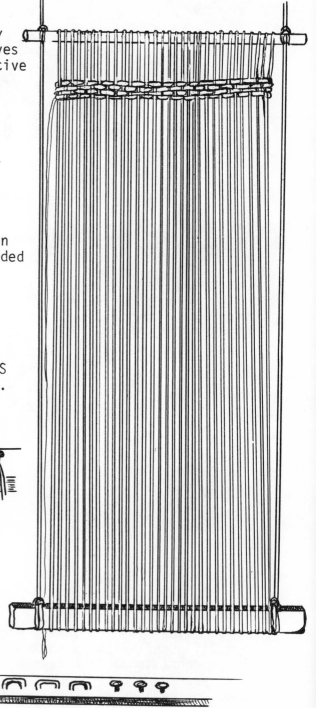

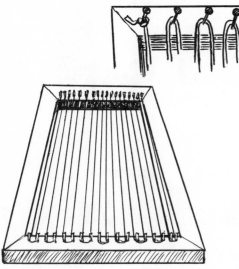

CANDLES

CANDLES can be used very effectively in Celebration, and are even more festive if they have been created specially for the occasion. It is difficult to make candles in groups. It takes a great deal of preparation and organization for the process of melting, pouring and cooling the wax. It is usually more satisfactory to make the candles at home or buy them.

Decorating the candles, however, can be a delightful activity for a group. Wax is a flexible, yielding material. You can shape, press, carve, color, glue, pull or melt it, and it will retain the shape you give it. Colored moulding wax can add an infinite number of variations in texture designs.

Real candle artistry involves taking into consideration the purpose of the candle and its basic shape. The candle, like sculpture in the round, should be pleasing from every angle.

Another candle-decorating technique makes use of old wax crayons. Heat water in a shallow pan until it boils. Put the crayons into the water. They will melt, forming a thin surface of wax on the top of the water. Remove the pan from the heat and pour off the water. While the wax is still soft, cut it into small shapes. These pieces can be applied to ordinary candles. Hold each piece briefly over a flame and then press it to the candle surface. The pieces will remain on the candle after it dries, creating a mosaic effect.

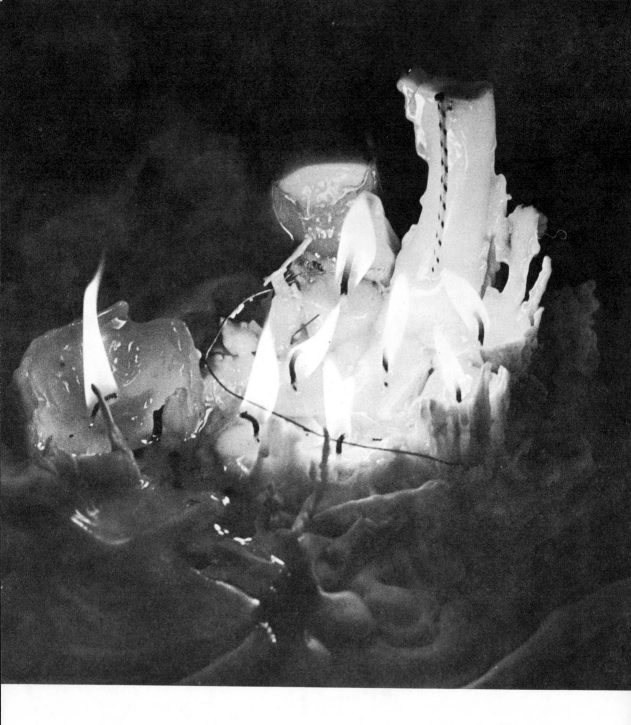

An indoor campfire was improvised for evening gatherings at an ecumenical workshop in Phoenix, Arizona. A cluster of old candles were wired together and set upon a plywood board. The low-burning candles became a focal point for the closing celebration. Individual candles had melted and merged, yet they retained their identity.

TORCHES

For outdoor, evening Celebrations, especially when the group is "on the move", TORCHES made with newspaper and paraffin can be a beautiful and very practical accompaniment. The TORCHES burn slowly and safely, with a bright flame.

All you will need to make them is:

wire hangers or sticks
newspaper
string
paraffin or old candles
a large can to melt wax

The base can be made with long sticks about 3/4 in. thick or with twisted coat hangers. The base should be about 24 in. to 30 in. long and rather sturdy.

Tear the newspaper into strips about 5 in. wide. Wrap the strips around one end of the base. You may need to tie or tape the ends of paper to the base. Wrap the roll or "log" of newspaper until it is about 3 in. thick, and 6 or 7 in. long.

Melt paraffin or old candles in a large tin can.

Caution: Wax is very inflammable. The can should be heated in boiling water rather than over an open fire.

Dip the newspaper "log" into the melted wax. Let the wax soak in so that the whole log is covered. When the wax has cooled the new torch is ready for use.

In one Celebration where these TORCHES were used, the group had a "torch-making party" the previous night. A song was written about the newspaper, "Gospel News on the Printed Page". The torches had even more meaning when they provided the only light for reading John I:1-9...

> *The Word had life in himself, and this life brought*
> *light to men. The light shines in the darkness, and*
> *the darkness has never put it out.*

WIRE SCULPTURE

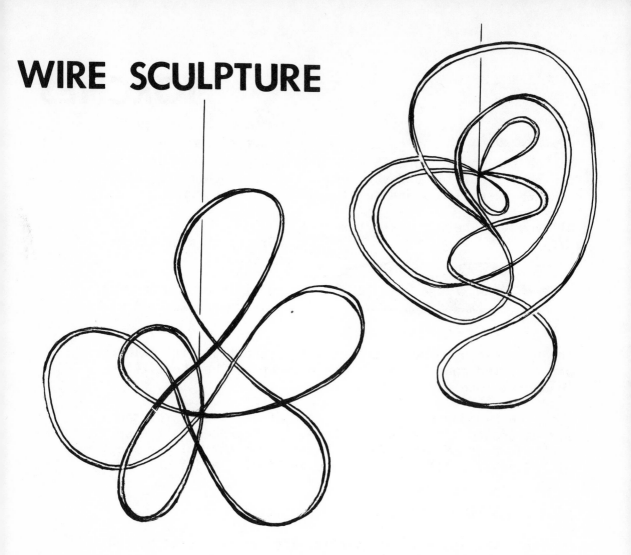

FREE-FORM WIRE SCULPTURES make beautiful mobile hangings for
special feasts. St. Thomas the Apostle Church in Hyde Park
used them as joyous Easter proclamations. The sculptures were
five to six feet in diameter. They were made with aluminum
wire 1/4 in. thick. Smaller ones could be made with lighter
gauge wire. The aluminum wire is light and can be formed into
graceful loopings without much difficulty.
When working with wire it is better to handle it as little as
possible. Too much bending makes the wire kinky.

WIRE SCULPTURE is a good activity for teamwork. It takes one
or two people to hold the shape, while a third person secures
the crossings and endings with light weight wire.

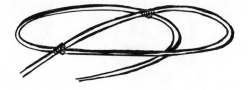

Brilliant colors of tissue paper can be glued to the wire
loops. This takes patience and care, but is well worth the
extra effort. When the wire sculptures are hung below lights,
they come alive and seem to shout out:

               "LIFT UP YOUR SPIRITS!
                HE IS RISEN!"

Another style of hanging sculpture is made with long sticks
of balsa wood and glue. Words or symbols of paper can be
worked nicely into the design.

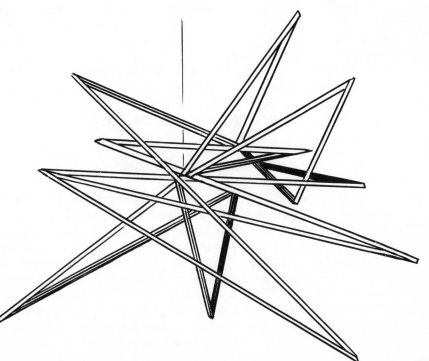

MASKS

There are many kinds of MASKS, and many reasons for wearing
them...
   the MASK you hide behind
      the MASK that blinds or limits your view of life,
         BLINDERS...

THE MASK THAT HELPS YOU PLAY A ROLE

   the MASK that reveals more of <u>you</u> than your own
                              face.

*A group of college students in Duluth, Minnesota,
became deeply engrossed in trying to probe the meaning
of the MASKS that they themselves wear. During part of
the closing sharing they painted faces on each other,
trying to let the painted face more fully reveal the
real person underneath. It is hard to describe the mixture of fun and sincere growth that took place. They sang
a song which they had written for the "washing of faces":*

> *WHO ARE YOU?*
> *I WANT TO KNOW.*
> *DARE TO BE FREE*
> *AND LET YOURSELF SHOW!*

*Another workshop group designed MASKS in a collage
manner. These MASKS represented the things which prevented
a total view of human existence. Such abstract things as:
FEAR, DESIRE FOR THE GOOD LIFE, PREJUDICE, INDIFFERENCE,
COMPETITION, HECTIC ACTIVITY, became visualized in concrete
images which actually obscured full vision when the MASKS
were worn. These MASKS were offered in the Confessing part
of the Mass with a prayer for the gift of whole vision and
courage to face the broader, but less secure view.*

BUTTONS

A BUTTON is an expression of who
I am and what I believe in.

It is a small BANNER that I can
wear, an extension of myself.
It travels with me.

A BUTTON makes a statement,
      invites conversation.
   It might even be a RISK.

When a BUTTON is used in a
 Celebration it should be an
integral part of the experience.
It could re-iterate a memorable
image or phrase, part of a song
or liturgical response. Like
 the bulletin cover, it helps
create the greeting environment.
A BUTTON is a tangible
          invitation to belong.
It says,
      "You are welcome."
      "Come, join a common
                  people."
Worn afterwards, it continues the
 Celebration. It says,
      "I was there."
      "I affirm the significance."

The BUTTON shown here was designed
specially for the Communion
Celebration of the United Church
of Christ, 8th General Synod, in
Grand Rapids. WHOLE EARTH WHOLE
PEOPLE was the centering image.

BULLETINS

The BULLETIN adds to the GREETING ENVIRONMENT. It is different from a program which lets you know what will be performed for you. The BULLETIN offers each person an opportunity to be a participant. When it can be originally created it speaks even more intensely that celebration is not a repeatable commodity, but a unique, sharing experience.

The BULLETIN can furnish a background understanding of the journey that will be taken. It can point up the significant stages of the journey, enabling you to participate fully. A carefully designed BULLETIN conveys the impression that something worth consideration has been prepared. Someone cares about your presence there. You are an important part of the event.

The BULLETIN COVER should not simply repeat a banner used, but perhaps expand a design or symbol. The bulletin, buttons, banners, sound and songs, responses, visual interpretations and dance should be an integrated whole that carries along the centering image of the celebration.

The BULLETIN COVER pictured here was reproduced by mimeograph stencil. Photographic stencils can be made from original drawings. This is much more economical than off-set printing, yet the result is quite professional. Covers can be printed by silkscreen or block-printing methods if the number desired is reasonable. Since each piece is handled individually, it is difficult to do more than 200 copies.

THE NAIL IS A SIMPLE MACHINE was a Celebration designed and offered by the Center for Contemporary Celebration during Holy Week. Each person, upon entering the church, was given a long, cut nail. This nail was used for an opening meditation. The tactile hardness and sharpness of the nail, plus all the related images of what a nail can do, made it a memorable symbol. This Crucifixion Celebration was a journey through the world of machines that man has produced-- machines which give man the power to shape or destroy life.

a nail is a simple machine

SILKSCREEN

The SILKSCREEN PROCESS is a method of print-making. The print is made by pulling a squeegee across the top of the silkscreen stencil and thus pressing the ink through the screen to the paper beneath. A true silkscreen or serigraph print makes use of several layers of over-lapping color and therefore the same print is run off several times with a different stencil for each color.

MATERIALS needed:

        Silkscreen - a frame with silk stretched across it tightly. The frame is attached to a flat board by hinges.

        Squeegee - a flat piece of rubber attached to a wooden handle, used to pull ink across the silkscreen.

        Silkscreen ink
        Silkscreen ink extender
        Turpentine or oleum
        Rags and newspaper
        Paper for printing

THERE ARE FOUR WAYS OF PREPARING THE SILKSCREEN STENCIL.

PROFILM STENCIL

1. MATERIALS: Profilm - a commercially made plastic-like, thin material attached to a heavy paper.
        Stencil knife
        Lacquer thinner

2. PROCESS:

With a stencil knife cut the design very carefully into the PROFILM, taking out those areas which are to be printed. Thus, the holes or negative areas cut away are the places the ink will go through on the screen and onto the paper print.

The PROFILM cut design is adhered to the silk by carefully rubbing it on with lacquer thinner. The lacquer thinner melts the PROFILM and attaches it to the screen.

CAUTION. Over-use of lacquer thinner will dissolve the whole design.

3. CHARACTER:
    Sharp lines, crisp edges, especially good for
    lettering.

TOUCHE STENCIL

1. MATERIALS: Brush
    Le Page's glue diluted with water
    Touche - an oily black substance which
        resists glue.
    Turpentine - does not effect glue, but
        dissolves touche.

2. PROCESS:
    The design is painted directly on the screen with
    touche and a brush. Lovely brush effects can easily
    be achieved with this method. The touche design
    must be allowed to dry over-night. When it is dry
    diluted Le Page's glue is squeegeed across the screen.
    The glue will fill the screen but will not stay on
    the touche painted areas. The glue should be left
    to dry for a few hours. The touche is then cleaned
    out with turpentine and a rag, leaving clear silk-
    screen in the areas to be printed.

3. CHARACTER:
    Feathery brushed line, good for small delicate
    detail and many stencils.

GLUE-OUT STENCIL

1. MATERIALS: Le Page's glue, diluted
    Brush

2. PROCESS:
    Paint your design directly on the screen, block-
    ing out areas which will not be printed.

3. CHARACTER:
    Fast, free brush-stroke effect

PAPER STENCIL

1. MATERIALS: Brown wrapping paper
              Stencil knife

2. PROCESS:
    Cut out design with stencil knife or scissors, or
    tear out the areas you wish printed. Attach this
    paper to the "underneath" side of the silkscreen
    with masking tape.

3. CHARACTER:
    Fastest method, soft edge, good for only limited
    printing.

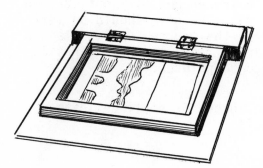

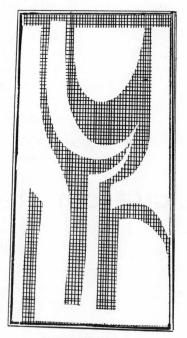

PAPER STENCIL

The SILKSCREEN PRINT on the next page
was made by using three different kinds
of stencils. The first two colors,
orange and pink, were printed with torn-
paper stencils. A cut-paper stencil
was used for the black. The tusche and
glue method, for the white.

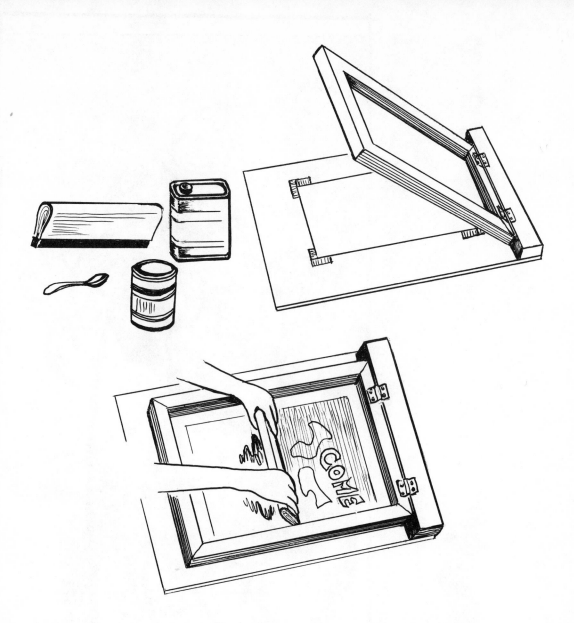

PRINTING After the silkscreen is prepared by of the me-
          thods described, the paper to be printed is
          placed under the screen and ink is pulled across
          the top of the screen with the squeegee. Each
          color printing is called a run. Mark the exact
          spot for placing the paper with a masking tape cor-
          ner. It will be necessary to key the print carefully
          for second and third color runs. The first experi-
          mental print with all first runs is called the
          Artist's Proof. Changes may be made before running
          the entire edition.

My heart is ready, God
    my heart is ready:

I mean to sing
        and play for you!

Awake, my muse,
Awake, lyre and harp,

I mean to
        wake the Dawn!

                    Psalm 57

Part 5   THE CHURCH YEAR

SEASONS AND DAYS OF CELEBRATION

Filled with an array of ideas, techniques and possibilities, the banner artist or group is ready to share time and talents with the parish liturgy team as they begin planning for coming feasts. The rhythm of the Church Year offers rich opportunities for creativity.

Ideally the well-organized liturgy team will begin planning the major events at least two months ahead of time. It is a great injustice to expect banner-makers to design and execute something significant in a week or two.

THANKSGIVING

The Church Year begins with Advent, but in practice most parishes try to make Thanksgiving weekend a time of special beauty in music, symbolism and community prayer, often joining ecumenically with neighboring churches. A new banner combined with attractive arrangements of harvest vegetables and fruits, cornstalks, dried weeds and fall flowers, creates an environment that fills our senses. All of these become images that evoke gratitude from the depths of our beings for the gifts of the earth. It is the careful interweaving of traditional with new images that makes the present feast alive and real.

ADVENT

In designing for liturgy, the banner artist must know not only what is beautiful and fresh, but what is capable of calling forth the community's prayer. What colors, textures, shapes, symbols will make Advent present within the worship space? What are the readings, hymns, devotions of the season? What are the lives of the people like at this time? What images will help them center their thoughts on the Advent experience?

For the last two years I have been involved with a parish liturgy team that has done just this kind of questioning. I would like to share briefly some of the ideas and environments that grew from the planning. Combined with the visual beauty, this parish places an equally high priority on excellence in word and music.

The candles in this banner are shades of gold, orange and deep red on a lighter gold background of drapery fabric.

FIRST SUNDAY OF ADVENT "God, for you I wait all the day."

    This is the time for waiting-- watching for the signs that tell us He is near. To "WATCH" includes a readiness to receive Him in whatever manner He may come to us.
Be on your guard, stay awake, because you never know when the time will come!

SECOND SUNDAY OF ADVENT   "Prepare the way for the Lord,
                          make straight His paths."
     Prophets see the necessity for change in a society. We must
   clear the way for change, continue the journey, open our
lives to receive Christ.

THIRD SUNDAY OF ADVENT "Rejoice! the Lord is near."

Our spirit quickens at the words of John announcing that a mighty savior is in our midst. John's message is good news. At the Lord's coming, those who are blind see, the crippled walk in the way of the Lord, the deaf hear his word and the dead rise to a life beyond imagining.

FOURTH SUNDAY OF ADVENT   "Rejoice so highly favored! The Lord
                                is with you."
This Sunday brings Advent's journey to a climax. Mary has
said, "YES" ...Her mission, which articulates the mission of
every Christian, is to give life, to bring Christ into the
world.

HOW THE BANNERS WERE USED

The key word for each Sunday of Advent was chosen by the planning group. The altar area of the church was kept unadorned except for two bare evergreen trees. The altar was covered with a purple cloth; pulpit and lectern stands, with simple purple hangings. One banner was carried in each Sunday as part of the Entrance Procession and placed in a waiting, free-standing holder. A very large Advent Wreath was beautifully situated in the center aisle and lighted as a part of the opening prayers. Each of the four priests used the key word and the banner as a theme for the homily. The homilies were different but carried the congregation through Advent with continuity. The mood of anticipation was heightened. It seemed as if everyone was waiting for the fourth banner to be in place.

For the Parish Reconciliation Service just before Christmas, all four banners were carried in procession and placed across the front of the altar area. It made an impressive closing to the Advent journey.

These banners were 52 in. wide and 9 ft. long. The background was a light purple suraline material with felt designs in dark purple and white. Deep rose was added to the Third Sunday banner. Blue and silver were added to the Mary banner for the Fourth Sunday of Advent.

ENVIRONMENTS

As the same liturgy group met to plan Advent a year later, a new approach was needed. We decided upon the image of a desert experience for the spiritual preparation time that Advent is meant to be. With the expertise of some very talented people, a desert environment was created to the left of the pulpit area. Beginning with milk crates, canvas, newspaper and vinyl drop clothes, to which was added a load of white sand, the desert was brought forth. A few desert plants gave it character. A photo cannot capture the actual feel of the setting. People responded very favorably to it.

The banner was designed to carry through the idea of journey to a quiet place, a place to find Christ within. The desert hills and pathway were cut with paper stencils and air brushed right on the sandy beige background. Something of the same effect could be achieved with soft chalk on stretched fabric. It would then need to be sprayed with fixative.

Advent environment at
St. Celestine Church,
Elmwood Park, Illinois

GLUE GUN

The words were added one at a time, begin-
ing with "COME", for each of the weeks of
Advent. I used an electric hot glue gun
to adhere the letters. It is such an easy
and quick way to glue fabric to fabric that I seldom use white
glue. The hot glue is bonded as soon as it cools, thus elimi-
nating long sewing time or long glue drying time. When carefully applied the letters and shapes lie more smoothly on the
backing

CHRISTMAS

I've done various kinds of banners for Christmas. Some have been designed in three segments. A snowflake-like star on a red velvet background makes a joyous statement. Another idea that worked well was abstract streams of light proclaiming the BURST OF CHRIST. However, with all the other Christmas decorations of flowers, candles and lighted trees, along with the manger scene, a banner may be too much.

The banner on this page was designed for a contemporary church in Chicago. The church is wedge-shaped. The architectural space calls for a large hanging banner as a central focus. This banner was ten feet by 30 feet, made of rich red background material. Large banners require very careful tailoring so that they will hang well. They can also become engineering problems.

*Lenten environment
at St Celestine Church,
Elmwood Park, Illinois*

LENT

Carrying through the idea of a meditation environment, the planning group decided to focus on a Lenten setting with a large,
rugged wooden cross, surrounded with harsh rocks and bare branches.
Gray, the color of sackcloth and ashes was chosen for the Lenten
color, instead of the royal purple which came in at a later time in
Church history.

The banner proclaimed:

CALLED TO A CHANGE OF HEART

It was displayed on the wall opposite the cross. It emphasized
the image of barren branches that held the possibility of new life.
Cards, the size of credit cards, printed with the banner design
and a Lenten prayer, were distributed to the congregation on the
First Sunday of Lent. The Parish Lenten Mission centered on the
idea of "CHANGE OF HEART".

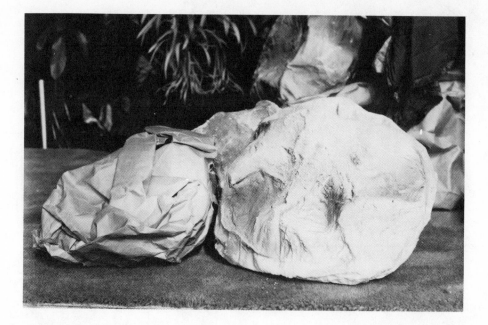

SIMULATED ROCKS

Actual rocks of the size needed for a large church sanctuary become a "weighty" problem. Simulated rocks can be made with brown paper grocery bags, plaster gauze bandages and spray paint.

Turn the bags inside out and shape them into various rock forms. The gauze covered with plaster is sometimes called "Pariscraft". Doctors use it to make casts. Dip the gauze strips into water for a few seconds and then drape them over the paper bag rock. Continue the process until the bag is covered. Let the plaster shape dry over-night. It is then ready to spray with gray, white, brown, beige etc. spray paint to create a motley rock effect. If you want lots of rocks, get a group together for a "ROCK PARTY". The rocks can be stored in boxes. They seem to improve with age.

HOLY THURSDAY

The Holy Thursday service was celebrated as a special dinner party. People were welcomed at the doors with a gracious sign. Just inside, at the back of the main aisle was a beautifully set banquet table with loaves of bread, centerpiece of grapes, lighted candles, red wine and goblets. Another similar arrangement was placed in front of the altar. The Lord's Supper became a new and solemn sharing of a meal.

118

Good Friday setting at St. Celestine Church,
Elmwood Park, Illinois

GOOD FRIDAY

The Cross and Branches environment of Lent had been removed
for the Holy Thursday liturgy. On Good Friday, a new design
was arranged to set the solemn tone of the day. With the
help of a carpenter, three crosses were erected. The piles
of rocks helped define the space. For the evening service,
the crosses were lighted with concealed red spot-lights. The
rest of the sanctuary was unadorned. The effect was a very
meditative and prayerful space.

EASTER

For the Easter liturgies, the cross was moved to the back center
position and draped with graceful green cloth. The mound of rocks
was surrounded with growing plants and flowers. The space to the
left of the pulpit became the Baptismal area with a flowing fountain
living plants and Easter blossoms. The glorious Easter sun streamed
through the stained glass to complete the Resurrection environment.

EASTER

With the emphasis on NEW LIFE, LIGHT, the ENERGY of the SPIRIT, WATER, REBIRTH and RENEWAL, Easter should be a burst of springtime color, sunlight and bubbling water. The fragrance of the flowers joins with the Alleluias of the choir to live the Resurrection event now.

Easter environment at St. Celestine Church, Elmwood Park, Illinois

PENTECOST

After all the glory and color of Easter, the Feast of
Pentecost is often overlooked. This is the time to pro-
claim the presence of the Holy Spirit in the CHURCH, and
the mission of each baptized person. It is time for the
rich colors of fire and the dynamic energy of wind. To
acknowledge the action of the SPIRIT within each of us
is to accept the commission of spreading the Good News.

ORDINARY TIME

A banner for ordinary time can be a non-verbal expression of the growth and energy of the Kingdom of God. Fashioned in shades of green and white, with touches of yellow, the lines speak of life growing from a very small beginning.

Ordinary time draws us into the teachings and stories of Christ. A banner may sing of the joy of knowing Christ better, of being ready to follow as a true disciple. Another image might be the growth of FAMILY in CHRIST. Ordinary time does not mean things become boring. A fresh banner can help keep the vision alive.

A family banner made with blue denim and patchwork quilting.

FURTHER READING

AMERICA'S PICTORIAL QUILTS. Caron L Mosey. Paducah, Kentucky: American Quilter's Society, 1985. Beautifully illustrated in full color. The techniques described can easily be adapted to banner-making.

AWARD WINNING APPLIQUE TECHNIQUE. Wilma and Carolyn Johnson. Paducah, Kentucky: American Quilter's Society, 1985. Colorful illustrations show step-by-step procedures for creating with applique. Many helpful hints apply to the making of banners.

THE BANNER BOOK. Betty Wolfe. Connecticut: Morehouse Barlow Co., Inc., 1974. For the beginner at banner-making. Betty introduces basic ideas and includes illustrations and step-by-step directions with a large number of experiences.

BANNERS AND FLAGS. Margot Carter Blair and Cathleen Ryan. New York: Harcourt Brace Jovanovich, 1977. This comprehensive book comes highly recommended by Modern Liturgy art director George Collopy.

BANNERS AND HANGINGS: Design and Construction. Norman Laliberte and Sterling McIlhany. New York: Reinhold, 1966. Imaginative use of applique' and stitchery, buttons and bells.

BANNERS WITHOUT WORDS. Jill Knuth. San Jose, California: Resource Publications, Inc. 1985. You'll treasure this collection of 28 columns by Modern Liturgy's Jill Knuth. Inspiration, instruction and handy tips for making your own wordless banners.

BATIK: Art and Craft. Nik Krevitsky. New York: Reinhold, 1964. A clear and fascinating presentation of a variety of Batik techniques.

CANDLE-MAKING. Susanne Strose. New York: Sterling Publishing Co., Inc., 1968. Includes many decorating techniques as well as directions for making candles.

CONTEMPORARY BATIK AND TIE-DYEING. Donna Z. Meilach. New York: Crown Publishing Corporation, 1978. Further exploration of batik methods.

CRAYON TECHNIQUES. Reynolds Girdler, Jr. New York, Toronto, London, 1969. Explores the many beautiful effects that can be achieved with crayons.

CREATING VISUAL IMAGERY IN WORSHIP. Rosemary Brown. Nashville, Tenn: Abingdon Press, 1986. Illustrations and diagrams show a variety of environment set-ups using visual imagery from Scriptures and from experiences of Life. Rev. Brown combines altar area settings with further ideas for music, texts and sermon suggestions carefully inter-woven.

DECORATIVE WALL HANGINGS: Art with Fabric. David B. Van Domelan. New York: Funk and Wagnalls Co., 1962. Explains and illustrates techniques in applique, stencil, batik, hooking, stitching, etc.

DESIGN ON FABRIC. Meda Parker Johnston ad Glen Kaufman. New York: Reinhold, 1967. Explains and illustrates all forms of fabric decoration. It is especially fine on batik and tie-dye.

ECCLESIASTICAL CRAFTS. Bucky King and Jude Martin. New York: Van Nostrand Reinhold Company, 1978. A beautifully illustrated book for the professional artist who wishes to gain greater understanding of the needs of churches and synagogues in the fine crafts of textile, wood, metal, and ceramics.

ENVIRONMENT AND ART IN CATHOLIC WORSHIP. Bishops' Committee on the Liturgy. Washington: USCC, 1978. A fundamental document not only for matters of art and architecture but for understanding the basic importance of the assembly.

FABRIC COLLAGE. Anna Ballarian. Worcester, MA: Davis Publications, Inc. 1976. Advanced techniques in contemporary stitchery and applique including some soft sculpture ideas that would add new life to a banner-making group.

FIBER EXPRESSION: KNOTTING AND LOOPING. Sarita R. Rainey. Worcester, Mass: Davis Publications, Inc., 1979. A delightful book for those interested in adding 3-dimensional symbols or pattern to non-verbal banners.

THE HOLY WEEK BOOK. Edited by Eileen E. Freeman. San Jose, CA: Resource Publications, Inc., 1979. This major resource book will help you plan more creative Holy Week liturgies. It treats each special day of Holy Week in detail, providing historical background, liturgical theology, creative ideas and practical examples.

HOW TO CREATE BANNERS. Virginia Broderick and Judi Bartholomew. New York: Costello Publishing Company, Inc. 1977. A handbook on how to make banners. It is also an idea book which will add to your vocabulary of symbols, designs, and materials.

LITURGY WITH STYLE AND GRACE. Revised Edition. Gave Huck. Chicago, IL: Liturgy Training Publications, 1984. Archdiocese of Chicago, 155 East Superior St., Chicago, IL 60611. A basic manual for planners and ministers. This book is an introduction and a refresher course for persons involved in liturgical ministry.

PARISH PATH THROUGH ADVENT AND CHRISTMASTIME. Edited by Mary Ann Simcoe. Chicago, IL: Liturgy Training Publications, 1983. Articles on the scriptures, prayers, music, gestures and environment of the winter seasons.

PARISH PATH THROUGH LENT AND EASTERTIME. Edited by Mary Ann Simcoe. Chicago, IL: Liturgy Training Publications, 1984. Second edition of this book has articles, on the lectionary, sacramentary, music and environment of these seasons.

SAINTS, SIGNS, AND SYMBOLS. W. Ellwood Post. New York: Morehouse-Barlow Co., 1974. A handbook rich in background on the many signs and symbols in Christian tradition.

SCREEN PRINTING: CONTEMPORARY METHODS AND MATERIALS. Frances and Norman Lassiter. Philadelphia, Penn: Hunt Manufacturing Co., 1978. This book is designed as a standard text for silk screening. It is understandable, instructional and motivational. It covers the various stencil techniques in light of the most recent technological advances in materials and procedures.

SYMBOLS OF CHURCH SEASONS AND DAYS. John Bradner. New York: Morehouse-Barlow Co., 1977. An illustrated compendium of practical symbols for use during the liturgical year.

TEXTILE ART IN THE CHURCH. Marion Ireland. Nashville, TN: Abingdon Press, 1966. Full color illustrations present an array of elegant and artistically crafted hangings and vestments.

WALL HANGINGS: Designing with Fabric and Thread. Sarita R. Rainey. Worcester, MA: Davis Publications, Inc. 1971. For those interested in pursuing intricate creating with needle and thread.

INDEX

Dear mouse friends,
Welcome to the world of

Geronimo Stilton

P9-BZI-879

THE RODENT'S GAZETTE
EDITORIAL STAFF

Geronimo Stilton
A learned and brainy
mouse; editor of
The Rodent's Gazette

Thea Stilton
Geronimo's sister and
special correspondent at
The Rodent's Gazette

Trap Stilton
An awful joker;
Geronimo's cousin and
owner of the store
Cheap Junk for Less

Benjamin Stilton
A sweet and loving
nine-year-old mouse;
Geronimo's favorite
nephew

Geronimo Stilton

RUMBLE IN THE JUNGLE

Scholastic Inc.

If you purchased this book without a cover, you should be aware that this book is stolen property. It was reported as "unsold and destroyed" to the publisher, and neither the author nor the publisher has received any payment for this "stripped book."

No part of this publication may be reproduced, stored in a retrieval system, or transmitted in any form or by any means, electronic, mechanical, photocopying, recording, or otherwise, without written permission from the copyright holder. For information regarding permission, please contact: Atlantyca S.p.A., Via Leopardi 8, 20123 Milan, Italy; e-mail foreignrights@atlantyca.it, www.atlantyca.com.

ISBN 978-0-545-48193-9

Copyright © 2011 by Edizioni Piemme S.p.A., Corso Como 15, 20154 Milan, Italy.

International Rights © Atlantyca S.p.A.

English translation © 2013 by Atlantyca S.p.A.

GERONIMO STILTON names, characters, and related indicia are copyright, trademark, and exclusive license of Atlantyca S.p.A. All rights reserved. The moral right of the author has been asserted.

Based on an original idea by Elisabetta Dami.

www.geronimostilton.com

Published by Scholastic Inc., 557 Broadway, New York, NY 10012. SCHOLASTIC and associated logos are trademarks and/or registered trademarks of Scholastic Inc.

Stilton is the name of a famous English cheese. It is a registered trademark of the Stilton Cheese Makers' Association. For more information, go to www.stiltoncheese.com.

Text by Geronimo Stilton
Original title *Grosso guaio in Mato Grosso*
Cover by Giuseppe Ferrario (design) and Giulia Zaffaroni (color)
Illustrations by Giuseppe Ferrario (design) and Giulia Zaffaroni (color)
Graphics by Chiara Cebraro

Special thanks to AnnMarie Anderson
Translated by Lidia Morson Tramontozzi
Interior design by Kay Petronio

12 11 10 9 8 7   14 15 16 17 18/0

Printed in the U.S.A.   40
First printing, April 2013

MY NAME IS GERONIMOOOOOOO!

Hello, dear rodent friends! Allow me to introduce myself. My name is Stiltoooooon! Geronimoooooooo Stiltoooooooooooon!

I'm so sorry to introduce myself in such a rude way. I'm usually a **calm** and **peaceful** rodent with a **calm** and **peaceful** desk

Heeeeeeelp!!!

job in a **calm** and **peaceful** office in New Mouse City, the capital of Mouse Island.

You're probably wondering why such a **calm** and **peaceful** mouse is holding on for dear life as his *SPEEDING* all-terrain vehicle zooms through a Brazilian rain forest. Actually, I'm asking myself the same thing! For the love of all things cheesy, what am I doing?

The rain forest is full of **DANGEROUS** animals — I'm surrounded by untamed *nature*! What was I thinking? As you might have guessed, I'm in the middle of another one of my incredible adventures.

It started on an evening like any other evening....

HELLO FROM BRAZIL!

It was a peaceful evening and I was relaxing at home. I was sprawled out on my favorite pawchair next to the fireplace, sipping a cup of HOT chocolate. I put on my COZY slippers and the new yellow robe my aunt Sweetfur had given me. I was listening to *classical* music and checking my email on the computer. Suddenly, a new message popped up on the screen! Who could it be from?

When I opened the *email*, a photo of a tropical rain forest appeared. In the picture, I saw a ferocious-looking snake, an **alligator**, and a hungry-looking PIRANHA . . . yikes!

How scary! There was a message attached to the photo:

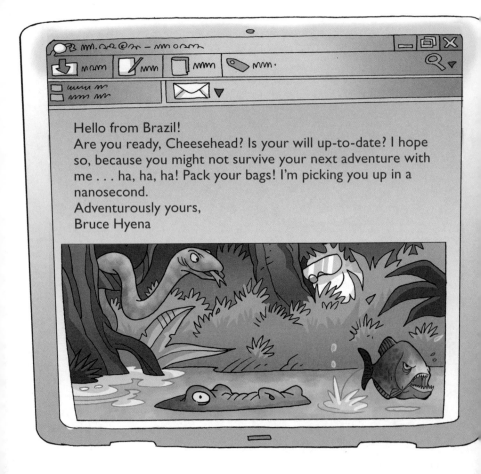

Hello from Brazil!
Are you ready, Cheesehead? Is your will up-to-date? I hope so, because you might not survive your next adventure with me . . . ha, ha, ha! Pack your bags! I'm picking you up in a nanosecond.
Adventurously yours,
Bruce Hyena

A second later, the doorbell rang.

DING DONG! DING DONG!

I JUMPED out of my chair, choking on my hot chocolate. In the process, I spilled the hot chocolate everywhere, staining my new robe. If that wasn't enough, my eyeglasses SLIPPED OFF my snout. For the love of cheese, I couldn't see a thing!

I heard a voice on the other side of the door shout, "Geronimooooooo! Are you ready, Cheesebrain?"

I STAGGERED toward the door, stumbling around in a total fog. Then I tripped on the rug, did a triple somersault, and landed headfirst in my little red fish Hannibal's glass bowl.

HOW I ENDED UP IN HANNIBAL'S BOWL!

4

Where am I?!

I staggered toward the door, stumbling around in a total fog . . .

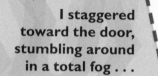

5

Ahhhh!

. . . I tripped on the rug and did a triple somersault . . .

Glub!

???

. . . and landed headfirst in Hannibal's bowl.

6

ARE YOU READY, CHEESEHEAD?

The door **burst** open, and someone almost ran me over.

"Are you ready, Cheesehead?" the mouse **shouted** at me.

I wanted to ask, "Ready for what?" but instead it came out as "**GLUB!**"

Someone grabbed the bowl, and I heard him say, "You really are a **Cheesehead**, Geronimo!"

The mouse pulled the **bowl** off my head and I spit out the **water**. Then I stumbled around looking for my spare pair of glasses. After I found them, I **QUICKLY** checked to see if Hannibal was okay.

When I was sure my little **fish** was

swimming happily in his bowl again, I turned to see who had caused the **trouble**. A mouse as **massive** as a wardrobe and as **muscular** as a bodybuilder stood in front of me. He was **GRINNING** like a rodent who had just heard the funniest joke! He wore **MIRRORED** sunglasses, but I recognized him immediately. It was my friend **BRUCE HYENA**! Do you know him? He's the most **adventurous** mouse on Mouse Island. There's even an entire page in the *Encyclopedia of Adventure* *dedicated* to him!

Glub!

THE ENCYCLOPEDIA OF ADVENTURE

NAME: Bruce Hyena

NICKNAME: Hyena

FAVORITE FOOD: Pizza

WHAT HE LOVES BEST: Nature

WHAT HE BELIEVES: That every rodent should follow his dreams!

HIS DREAM: That one day, there will be peace in the world!

HIS FEARS: Absolutely nothing at all!

HIS CHARACTERISTICS: He always survives, wherever and whenever!

HIS STRENGTH: Leading a group on an adventure.

HIS WEAKNESS: He's secretly a mushy sentimentalist. And he has a big crush on Thea Stilton!

HIS FAVORITE SPORT: He loves every sport, but he especially enjoys parachuting, triathlons, and other extreme sports.

OTHER INTERESTS: He reads poetry!

Bruce smiled brightly. "Hey, Cheese Puff, are you ready?" he asked.

"Huh? R-ready for what?" I STAMMERED.

"There's no time to explain!" Bruce said hurriedly. "You'll figure it out eventually! Now, enough talk . . . let's get busy!"

As quick as lightning, he turned to my computer, clicked on the email icon, typed in my password (How did he know it? That's supposed to be TOP SECRET!), and went into my inbox! He pointed to the message with the photo of the snake, the PIRANHA, and the alligator.

"Did you see this email?" he asked. "Are you ready?"

"I don't know what I'm supposed to be ready for!" I exclaimed in frustration. "And how did you get into my email?"

"Easy, cheesy," Bruce said with a chuckle. "I know your **PaSSWORD**, Cheesehead!"

"But that's supposed to be **TOP SECRET**!" I practically shouted.

He waved his cell phone under my snout.

"The other day, I accidentally — ahem, well, almost accidentally — **FILMED** you as you were typing the password. So now I know it! Your password is '**cheese**.' Sorry to say it, Cheesehead, but that's an **EXTREMELY EASY** one. You really should choose something a bit more **DiFFiCULt**. Don't you know anything about Internet **SECURITY**?"

"But I —" I started to reply, but Bruce cut me off.

"No time for chitchat!" he said as he logged in to my personal **Mousebook** page (using my secret password **AGAIN**!). He typed **FURIOUSLY** for a few seconds, and when I looked at the screen, he had **DELETED** everything I had ever posted!

"You erased **EVERYTHING**?" I exclaimed. I was so exasperated and UPSET that I passed out from the *shock*.

THE MOST AWESOME
MOUSE EVER!

I came to because someone threw a pail of **cold** water on my snout. I opened my eyes and saw him again. It wasn't a **NIGHTMARE**. Bruce was still standing in the middle of my living room.

"Aren't you going to **thank** me?" he asked. "Aren't you happy I **DELETED** your Mousebook page? I did it for your own good, Cheesehead!"

"My own good?" I asked, **PERPLEXED**.

"Don't look at me like that, Cheesehead!" Bruce said. "Your **Mousebook** page was **BORING**! All of your photos show a mouse in *elegant* jackets with **starched** shirts and **STUFFY** ties.

"You're always sitting in a **BORING** office, and you only post about **BORING** things like books and antique cheese rinds. **BORING**! It was like any other Mousebook page."

"But I —" I began to protest, but Bruce cut me off *again*!

"Don't worry, Cheesehead!" he said with a **WILD** smile. "I have the solution! I'm going to replace your **BORING** old photos with some incredible action shots. Your Mousebook page will be **awesome** instead of **BORING**, and you'll be the *most awesome mouse ever*!"

"But I am a **BORING** mouse!" I exclaimed. "We've known each other for such a long time, Bruce. You already know I'm a boring intellectual! I'm a **shy** rodent who loves a quiet life! I'm not **VERY** adventurous,

or **VERY** awesome, or even a little bit awesome! I'm just a shy, **VERY** frightened mouse!"

Bruce slapped his paw on my shoulder so hard I winced.

"Don't worry, Cheesehead, I'll take care of that," he said. "You'll see. Soon your Mousebook page will be full of EXTREMELY adventurous photos!"

Then he grabbed the phone.

"Hi, is that you?" he asked. "Yeah, it's me. She's there, too? Is everything ready? Great! He's set to be picked up! What are you talking about? He's not going to refuse. **HA, HA, HA!** I just erased his Mousebook page and I'm holding all his archived EMAILS hostage. Keep the helicopter's motor warm, the snakes' antivenom cold, and prepare his last will and testament! In other words,

keep everything ready! See you later!"

He hung up and **SMILED** at me.

"Know who I was talking to? It was —"

An extremely **LOUD** noise, like a helicopter **FLYING** over my house, drowned out his words. In fact, it actually *was* a helicopter! An instant later, someone opened a **trapdoor** in the attic (which I didn't even know existed!) and came down a ROPE!

Slimy Swiss cheese!

A rodent with a bright

smile and magnetic **jade-green** eyes landed in front of me with an *agile* leap.

I recognized him immediately. It was **Wild Willie**, also known as **WW**! What was he doing in my living room? I didn't have time to answer my own question because another rodent with an even brighter smile and **penetrating** eyes as **black** as coal landed with a **GRACEFUL** jump at his side. It was his cousin Maya! I barely knew her.

What was happening?

Bruce greeted them with **VIGOROUS** handshakes.

"Take lots of **PHOTOS** and make sure there are lots of **ADVENTURES**, okay?" he told them. "Snakes, alligators, spiders, and, as long as you're there, **scorpions**, too. They always make for a **GOOD SHOW!**"

"You can count on it!" Wild Willie answered as he gave Bruce one of his super-intense **LOOKS**. "Don't worry. By the time he gets back, this **rookie** will have the most **ADVENTUROUS** photos on **Mousebook**! They'll be photos that will make every mouse **wildly** jealous — well, if he comes back *alive*, that is!"

Before I could squeak a response, Wild Willie, Maya, and Bruce tied my belt to a **strange** contraption, and in an instant, I was pulled up

into the air like a bag of cheese puffs.
Zuuuuuuup!

I **zipped** out through the attic window, **over** my roof, and up to a helicopter.

As I was hoisted aboard, Bruce **SHOUTED** to me from below.

"You'll see, **Cheesehead**, you'll have lots of fun! A trip in the most **ADVENTUROUS** country in the world awaits: You're going to **BRAZIL**! And you'll come back with the most **amazing** photos ever!"

"Wh-why aren't you coming with us?" I **shouted** back with a stammer.

"I can't!" he replied in a **BOOMING** voice. "I'm competing in the Parachuting World Championship. Wild Willie and Maya will take care of you. **RELAX!** You're in good hands. And remember, Cheesehead: When they take your picture, **smile!**"

DESTINATION: ADVENTURE!

The helicopter **WHiRLED** toward the airport at **WARP** speed. We boarded a **LARGE** plane headed nonstop to Brazil.

It was a **very LONG** trip. You probably know Brazil is located in South America, but you probably don't know how **far** it is from New Mouse City. Let me tell you, it's really, really **far**!

Wild Willie sat on my right, and Maya was on my left. As the plane took off, Wild Willie opened a **tourist guide** to Brazil and began to read.

"Hey, rookie," he said, "Did you know that **Brasília**, Brazil's capital, is very **MODERN**? It didn't even exist before

1956, when it was built. And it officially became the capital of Brazil in 1960. If you look down on the city from above, it's shaped like an AIRPLANE!"

I tried to make an INTELLIGENT remark, but Wild Willie continued without pausing, "You know, rookie, in just a few days Rio de Janeiro will host the most famouse CARNIVAL in the entire world."

Destination . . . Adventure!

???

DESTINATION: BRAZIL!

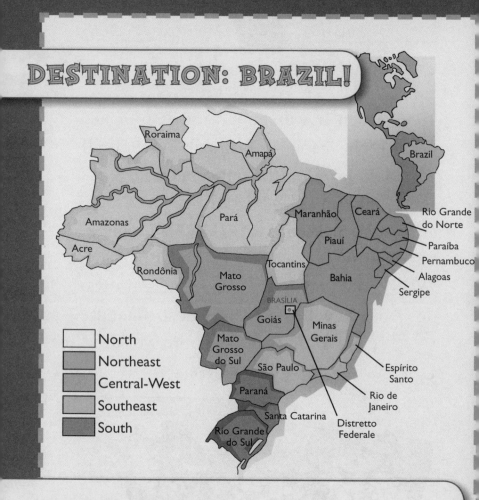

Roraima
Amapá
Brazil
Pará
Maranhão
Ceará
Rio Grande do Norte
Amazonas
Piauí
Paraíba
Pernambuco
Acre
Alagoas
Rondônia
Tocantins
Sergipe
Mato Grosso
Bahia
BRASÍLIA
Goiás
Minas Gerais
Mato Grosso do Sul
São Paulo
Espírito Santo
Paraná
Rio de Janeiro
Santa Catarina
Distretto Federale
Rio Grande do Sul

North
Northeast
Central-West
Southeast
South

Location: South America

Capital: Brasília

Area: Brazil covers 3,287,612 square miles.

Population: More than 196 million people

Official Language: Portuguese

Characteristics: Brazil is the home of many natural wonders, such as the Amazon rain forest, which makes up more than half of the world's remaining rain forests.

"That's awesome!" Maya exclaimed. "It's impossible to get bored in Brazil! The country is rich in man-made and natural wonders: We'll tour the Iguazu Falls, the Amazon rain forest, and even the Pantanal! That's a tropical wetland that hosts lots of different plants and animals. There are snakes, spiders, alligators, and even piranhas!"

Juscelino Kubitschek Bridge in Brasília

"Snakes? Spiders? Alligators? Piranhas?" I asked. I was beginning to PANIC. "I want to go HOOOOOOOME!"

Iguazu Falls

Wild Willie pretended he hadn't heard me.

"Rookie, did you know that Brazil is full of *fazendas*, or

Jabiru bird

farms, where livestock are raised and COCONUT TREES, Bananas, PAPAYAS, PineaPPLes, SUGAR CANE, and citrus fruit are grown? We'll visit my friends Joao and Ana's *fazenda*. Excited yet?"

All those facts were making my head Spin.

After a while, Wild Willie and Maya's voices started to FADE, and my eyelids became **heavier** and **heavier**.

But Wild Willie continued chattering in my ear.

"Rookie, did you know there are LOTS of indigenous people living in Brazil, including my friends the Bororo?" He went on and on.

Maya, on the other hand, was trying to TEACH me Portuguese, the language spoken in Brazil.

But I wasn't listening anymore. I closed my **EYES** and was lulled to **SLEEP** by the drone of the plane's motor.

I DON'T UNDERSTAND ANYTHING!

I was awakened by a **female** mouse's voice speaking an unfamiliar language.

"Bem-vindo ao Brasil, senhor!"*

It was the flight attendant. When she realized I didn't **understand**, she used hand gestures to tell me I had to **get off** the plane.

Bem-vindo ao Brasil!

* *"Bem-vindo ao Brasil, senhor!"* means "Welcome to Brazil, sir!"

We had landed in Brazil! I looked around me and realized I was alone. "Wild Willie! Maya!" I SHOUTED, panicking. "Where are you?"

I wanted to ask the flight attendant if she had seen them leave, but I didn't know the language!

Why, why, oh why hadn't I learned Portuguese?

Maya had tried to teach it to me during the flight, but I had fallen asleep like a fool!

Why, why, oh why hadn't I forced myself to stay awake?

The flight attendant kept StaRiNG at me, so I got off the plane. I went out into the AIRPORT and looked around, hoping to find Maya and Wild Willie in the crowd.

Where had they gone?

I couldn't find them anywhere. The airport

1. International airport
2. Zoo
3. Stadium
4. Meteorological observatory
5. Hospital
6. TV tower
7. National theater
8. Cathedral
9. Itamaraty Palace
10. National Congress
11. Alvorada Palace
12. University of Brasília

Brasília replaced Rio de Janeiro as the capital of Brazil in 1960. The new capital city was built on a massive plateau in the State of Goiás, which is located in the center of the country. The Brazilian architect Lúcio Costa designed Brasília in the shape of an airplane to signify the city's readiness to fly into the future. Every area in the city has a particular function. For example, the city's major monuments, attractions, and government buildings are located within the body of the airplane, while stores and homes are found in the wings. The Brazilian capital is the only UNESCO World Heritage Site city built in the twentieth century.

security guard kept *staring* at me, so I left the airport and started to walk. I walked and walked. **Holey cheese!** There was so much to see. Brasília was a truly MARVEMOUSE city!

I began to search for Wild Willie and Maya in all the public **parks**, **streets**, and **tourist attractions** in Brasília. I walked through the city far and wide until my paws were so **tired** and **HOT** they started to smoke! In a final desperate move, I even climbed a very **tall** television tower, though I have a fear of **HEIGHTS**. But they weren't there, either!

With my tail between my legs, I came down the tower feeling **DEJECTED** and *sad*. I was a **lonely** mouse in an unfamiliar city. What was I going to do? Suddenly, my heart JUMPED. Through the crowd, I thought I saw a rodent wearing a **wide-brimmed** hat. Holey cheese, it looked just like Wild Willie's **hat**! I tried to catch up to the rodent, but I slipped on the WET sidewalk.

I *SLID* the entire length of the sidewalk, did a triple somersault through the air, and fell to the ground with a loud **thud**.

An ambulance took me to the hospital. I tried to explain what had happened, but no one could understand me, and I

Aaahhh!

Wild Willie!

Whoa!

couldn't **understand** them, either!

Why, why, oh why hadn't I learned Portuguese?

After my trip to the hospital, there was one thing I did understand, though. I had sprained a paw. (It was very, very **PAINFUL**!)

I also was beginning to understand that I probably wasn't going to find my **friends** in Brasília. I remembered they had talked about RIO DE JANEIRO. Maybe that's where they had **HEADED**. . . .

CARNIVAL IN RIO!

I bought a plane **ticket** and took the first flight to Rio de Janeiro. While I was in line to board the plane, I had the **sensation** that I was being followed. How **odd**!

A **surprise** awaited me in Rio. The **carnival** had begun! As soon as I got off the plane, I was overwhelmed by a jubilant crowd **singing** and *dancing* the

samba as they followed very **bright** and **cheerful** floats moving slowly down the streets.

I tried to get away from the crowds, but it was impossible. The dancing rodents **DRAGGED** me into the thick of things like a rushing river! At one point, I again had the **sensation** that I was being followed. In fact, I was positive I felt someone tug my **Jacket**! But when I turned around quickly, I didn't see anything suspicious.

After hours and hours in that throng of rodents, I saw a **SIGN** for a hotel. I hurried in and tried to get a room for the night. But no one could **UNDERSTAND** me, and I didn't **UNDERSTAND** anything, either.

Why, why, oh why hadn't I learned Portuguese?

I was finally able to communicate with gestures.

The following morning I went down to the hotel lobby to **pay** for my room. But when I reached for my credit card, I almost

had a heart attack. My wallet was no longer in my **pocket**! The hotel **manager** was very **ANNOYED**. He grabbed me by the ear and said something to me in Portuguese. Even though I didn't **UNDERSTAND** the language, I could tell he meant something like: *"You wanted to have a vacation for free, huh? Dream on! You're going to pay every cent you owe, penny by penny!"*

The hotel manager passed me over to the **cook**. The cook didn't need any words to communicate . . . he just showed me the sinkful of dirty dishes. I washed and washed and washed for the entire day. But that wasn't all. I had to unload the **LUGGAGE** and make all the **beds**! By nightfall, I thought I had paid off my debt. But the **BEST** was yet to come. With a big kick under my tail, the cook sent me back to the kitchen. He turned

Kick!

Samba?

Sambaa?

Sambaaa?

on some lively music and began showing me the steps to the **samba**.

"*Um e dois! Um e dois! Um e dois!*" The cook counted in Portuguese.

He made me WIGGLE and sway over and over again.

I couldn't figure out why he wanted me to learn the **samba**, but I tried my best. Too bad I don't have a sense of RHYTHM! As far as the WIGGLE and sway was concerned, no matter how hard I tried, I just couldn't do it. When it comes to dancing, I have **two left paws**!

After what seemed like an eternity, the cook dragged me out of the hotel. A **HUGE** Carnival float was waiting.

Finally, I understood why the cook had taught me to **samba**. I was going to have to ride on the float through one of the Carnival parades, **dancing** the samba the entire time! The cook urged me to get onto the float.

What else could I do?

So I climbed on board, and the float began to move into the crowded streets. I danced the **samba** as well as I could, but I was still really, really **TERRIBLE**.

How embarrassing!

The crowd seemed to enjoy my **dancing**, though, because they threw *coins* at me as a tip. **What good luck!** Maybe now I could pay for my hotel room and get out of Rio!

WHAT BEAUTIFUL WATERFALLS!

Luckily, it was the last day of the Carnival. The following morning at **DAWN**, my debts were paid and I was free to go. I counted the coins I had received as tips for my **TERRIBLE** samba dancing, and it was enough to buy an airplane **TICKET**. I decided to leave Rio to **LOOK** for Wild Willie and Maya in another place they had talked about: the **Iguazu Falls**!

Full of **HOPE**, I headed to the airport and bought a ticket to Foz do Iguaçu International Airport. Once I arrived there, I boarded an **overcrowded** bus brimming with tourists. When we finally got to the falls, I was overwhelmed.

Holey cheese, what a **FABUMOUSE** sight! The water from the river **tumbled** down from incredible heights, forming **swirling** eddies below. The noise the water made was a deafening **ROAR**. I was speechless. For an instant, I again had the feeling that I was being watched, and I had the distinct impression that someone was **FOLLOWING** me. But when I looked closely at the tourists around me, everyone looked perfectly normal. Was the cheese slipping off my **cracker**?

I scrutinized each face in the crowds around the falls, hoping to find Maya and Wild Willie. No luck! I quickly checked the parking lot, looking for them there. No luck! Then I peeked into every store, coffee shop, and souvenir stall I could find. **NO LUCK!** I even checked the bathrooms, but there wasn't even the SHADOW of my two friends.

With a sigh I went back to the pier and walked along the FOOTBRIDGE, where I could admire the falls a bit more closely. I stopped at a lookout point to enjoy the beautiful scenery.

I was just squeaking aloud about the falls when someone accidentally bumped into me — and I TUMBLED into the water!

"What beautiful waterfaaaaalls!"

The **RUSHING** current swept me under the falls. I tried desperately to get to the surface, but as soon as I came up, the **ENORMOUSE** swell of the water pushed me right under again with a **tremendous** crashing noise. It sounded like thousands of jackhammers drilling at the same time!

I finally came to the surface, gasping for air. I found myself in a calm pool at the foot of the **falls**. I bobbed in the water, looked around, and saw a boat coming closer to rescue me. **I was saved!**

I raised my arms and waved them wildly. "I'm alive!" I shouted. "I'll be fine! Everything is oka —"

But at that very moment, one of the **RESCUERS** threw a lifesaver at me. It hit me on my head so **hard** it knocked me under the water again.

GLUB!

I came up for air and whispered, "Great shot!"

Then I **FAINTED.**

Everything is oka —

Glub!

WHAT GOOD LUCK!

When I came to, I found myself in a hospital bed **AGAIN**! A polite doctor tried to tell me something, but I *couldn't understand* anything she was saying!

Why, why, oh why hadn't I learned Portuguese!

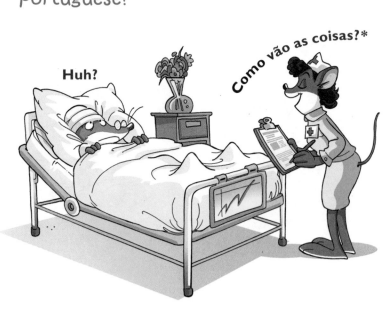

Huh?

Como vão as coisas?*

* *"Como vão as coisas?"* means "How is it going?"

Through hand gestures, the doctor made me understand I was a very **fortunate** mouse: I had survived falling over the Iguazu Falls with only an **ENORMOUSE** bump on my head! It could have been **MUCH, MUCH** worse!

After a few hours, I was discharged from the hospital and found myself again roaming the **STREETS** alone. I was miserable and didn't know what to do. Where were Wild Willie and Maya?

SUDDENLY, I remembered that in the plane they had spoken about the Pantanal, the largest tropical *wetland* in the world. I even remembered that their friends **Joao and Ana** lived on a *fazenda* in the Pantanal! Holey cheese, why didn't I think of it sooner! Wild Willie and Maya had to be there!

I went back to the airport to buy a **TICKET** to Cuiabá, the largest city and capital of Mato Grosso, the state where the Pantanal is located. Unfortunately, I didn't have any more **cash** (or my wallet), but I had become so **GOOD** at making myself understood with hand gestures that I was able to pay for the ticket directly from my bank account.

After a **SCARY** ride on a shaky plane, I landed in Cuiabá. As soon as I got out of the airport, I was immediately *surrounded* by a group of rodents vying to be my tour guide. Unfortunately, since all of my cash was gone, I had to settle for a lift on a truck packed with **sheep**. And the ride wasn't even free. I had to pay for it with my **WatCH**!

The **stinky** truck full of sheep bounced along the Transpantaneira, the long dirt road that crosses the Pantanal. The **stench** was **ATROCIOUS**!

After a couple of miles, the truck driver stopped and made me get off. Using hand gestures, he made me understand that he had **arrived** at his destination, so I had to proceed . . . on paw!

I tried to complain (after all, I had given him my **watch** to pay for the ride), but he didn't understand me.

Why, why, oh why hadn't I learned Portuguese!

So I began walking as the SUN set on the highway. I had been walking an hour or so, and I was losing hope of ever finding the *fazenda* when I saw a rodent on a horse riding toward me.

He was TALL and STRONG with shiny fur and eyes that sparkled. I sputtered out some words, trying to make myself understood.

"My name is Stilton, *Geronimo Stilton*," I squeaked. "*Fazenda* . . . Joao . . . Ana . . ."

He laughed loudly and pointed to himself.

"Thiago!"

By gestures, I understood he was one of Joao and Ana's friends. He also lived at the *fazenda*. WHat GOOD LUCK! After all my adventures, I couldn't believe my good fortune. Finally, something on this trip was going right!

Thiago helped me up onto the horse behind him, and together we RODE to Joao and Ana's. When I was introduced to Ana, I was delighted to find she spoke English. I was finally able to ask someone for some **news** about Wild Willie and Maya!

But to my dismay, my friends were not at the *fazenda,* and Joao and Ana hadn't heard from them, either. I was so **DEPRESSED** I could have cried!

Ana understood immediately and tried to cheer me up by offering a delicious treat she had prepared with her own hands: *manjar branco**. The WHISKER-LICKING GOOD pudding immediately put me in a good mood!

* *Manjar branco* is coconut pudding, a traditional Brazilian dessert.

MANJAR BRANCO

Ingredients for pudding:
4 cups whole milk
1 cup coconut milk
1 cup sugar
½ cup cornstarch
1 teaspoon vanilla extract

Ingredients for syrup:
½ cup sugar
½ cup water
1 cup pitted dried prunes

Combine the whole milk, coconut milk, sugar, cornstarch, and vanilla in a small pot. With an adult's help, place the pot on the stove on medium heat and mix the ingredients with a wooden spoon until the mixture thickens, about 15 minutes. Grease a bunting pan with a drop of oil and pour the pudding into it. Let it cool and set in the refrigerator for three hours. To make the syrup, combine the sugar, water, and dried prunes in a small pot. With an adult's help, bring it to a boil. Reduce heat and simmer on low heat for 15 minutes. When the pudding is set, carefully invert it onto a plate. Garnish with the syrup, and enjoy sharing your dessert!

"Geronimo, why don't you stay here for a couple of days and **rest**?" Ana asked as I ate the *manjar branco.* "You could give us a hand with the chores on the *fazenda,* and while you're at it, you could also LEARN a little Portuguese. I'd be happy to teach you. And the FRESH AIR and healthy living will be good for you!"

I gladly accepted the invitation.

"Thank you!" I told Ana. "Actually, I'm **very tired**, and I really must learn some Portuguese. And yes, I'm sure the FRESH AIR will be good for me!"

But as usual, I didn't know what I was in for. . . .

Yum, yum, yummy!

Ooops!
I gathered the oranges in the fruit grove, but I fell down the ladder and into a patch of poison ivy. I couldn't stop scratching!
Ouchie!
I brushed the horses, but one stomped on my left paw.
Zzzzzzzzzzz!
By nightfall I was so exhausted I fell asleep on top of a fence…
SO MUCH FOR FRESH AIR AND HEALTHY LIVING!

VAMOOOOOOS!

At the *fazenda*, I learned to appreciate the hard work that goes into farming, and the beauty of the countryside as well. Thanks to Ana, I finally learned a little Portuguese. I felt so much more confident! Armed with this knowledge, I was ready to start off again in search of Wild Willie and Maya.

Ana and Thiago suggested I look for them in the Bororo villages in the heart of the Pantanal. I told Ana I wanted to leave the next day.

"Before you go, we'd like to take you to a restaurant," she told me. "What do you want to EAT?"

"Well, how about some local food?" I suggested.

Ana and Thiago exchanged an **ODD** look.

"Are you sure?" Ana asked. "Do you *really* want to taste local food?"

I was *puzzled*.

"Of course," I replied. "Why wouldn't I?"

They both cheered happily.

"Then *vamos**!" Thiago exclaimed.

Then they jumped into their **ALL-TERRAIN VEHICLE** as if they were being chased. I still had my paw on the door handle when Ana shifted into gear and took off like a **ROCKET**!

I clung desperately to the handle as we *sped* off. I opened my mouth to yell, but a **MOSQUITO** flew in and I started coughing nonstop instead.

Now do you understand why I was clinging for dear life to an all-terrain vehicle in the middle of the Brazilian forest at the beginning of this book?!

* *"Vamos!"* means "Let's go!"

Ana's vehicle **ZOOMED** down the dirt road, which was a nightmare of potholes and **MUD PUDDLES**. Holey Swiss cheese! I could hear her laughter through the window.

"I love to drive on **dirt** roads!" Ana squeaked cheerfully. "*Vamoooooooooooos!*"

The radio was blasting samba music and the car seemed to **sway** to the rhythm. I finally spotted a restaurant. PHEW! Ana abruptly stopped in front of it. I flew off the handle of the car, straight into a signpost. I hit it with a loud *thud*!

THUDDDDD!

When I climbed down from the **SIGNPOST**, I realized it read: **BEWARE, IT BITES!**

I didn't have time to ask for an explanation because a short rodent with **shiny** oiled WHiSKeRS pushed me inside the restaurant. It was **ANTÓN CHEFRAT**, the owner. I noticed he surreptitiously winked at Ana, and she winked back. Then he **LOOKED** me up and down and turned to Thiago.

"Hmm," he mumbled. "Do you think he can?"

"**HE'S GOT TO!**" Thiago answered.

Antón Chefrat shrugged and mumbled, "We'll see. . . ."

He shimmied to the kitchen to the rhythm of the **samba** beat playing on the radio and returned with a steaming dish in one hand and a **STRANGE** entrée in the other.

"What did you **bring** me?" I asked curiously.

"Be quiet and eat!" he ordered.

So I began **EATING** as the three of them stared at me.

I felt very embarrassed.

"Why are you staring at me?" I asked. "What am I eating?"

Antón just **grinned**.

"Yummy! Not bad," I said as I finished eating and licked my whiskers. "In fact, it was really **good**! So tell me: What did I eat?"

"The first dish was **piranha** soup," Antón said with another grin. "And the second one was **ALLIGATOR** tail!"

I was about to **FAINT**, but I didn't have a chance.

"Before you leave, we **ABSOLUTELY** must take a keepsake **PHOTO**," my friends exclaimed excitedly as they pushed me out of the restaurant.

They dragged me to a shop next door. It was **long** and **narrow** with lots of glass display cases along its walls. I thought it was an **odd** place because even though it was a store, I couldn't figure out what it sold. The owner, a small and **SKINNY** rodent who was constantly laughing, came to **MEET** us. He started a long explanation in **PORTUGUESE**. He spoke very fast, so I couldn't understand a thing. At the end, he began giggling and repeating one word.

"Jibóia, jibóia, jibóia!"

Then he stretched out a hand in one of the display cases and took out a **HUGE** snake. It was the **longest** snake I had ever seen! Frozen feta, so that was the *jiboia*!

He placed it around my neck like a scarf as everyone talked all at once very **eXCiteDLy** and happily. Then he pulled out a camera and took my photo.

I turned as **PALE** as a slice of mozzarella.

"How do you say 'I'M ABOUT TO FAINT?' in Portuguese?" I asked Ana.

Finally, after taking about a million photos, they freed me from the snake!

I WON'T GET LOST!

The following day at DaWn, the time came for me to leave and continue the search for Wild Willie and Maya. Thiago and Ana explained how to get to the Bororo village deep in the Pantanal. Then they pointed to it on my map. It looked very simple and straightforward, and it wasn't too far from where we were. I figured I could walk there in only a few hours.

I said my thanks and farewells to my friends.

"Geronimo, are you sure you'll be able to find the ROAD to the village?" Ana asked with a serious face.

"Of course," I replied. "I'll be there before NIGHTFALL!"

"But are you sure you won't get lost?" Thiago asked. "The **RAINY** season has just ended and some paths may still be underwater. You might get *confused*!"

"Of course I won't get lost!" I replied. "I have the map you gave me, and it looks very SIMPLE!"

They just **shook** their heads.

"Well, just be sure not to be in the Pantanal after sunset," Ana warned. "It's **DANGEROUS**!"

"I won't get lost," I replied confidently. "I'm very **CONFIDENT**!"

I said good-bye and walked boldly down the path leading into the Pantanal. I had really become an *adventurous* mouse! Wild Willie and Maya would be so proud of me!

I entered the **FOREST**, and every so often stopped to check the road on the map. There were all sorts of amazing **MULTICOLORED** birds all around me. I decided to take a few **PHOTOS** to show my dear nephew Benjamin when I got home. I was so taken by everything that I didn't notice the **SUN** beginning to set. In no time at all, I found myself alone in the dark in the **heart** of the forest. It was exactly what Ana had told me to **AVOID**!

Only then did I understand how **foolish** I had been. I had been overconfident in my **abilities**, and I hadn't listened to those who loved me and had tried to warn me. As it got darker, **TERRIFYING** sounds filled the **NIGHT** air.

I took refuge under a tree and began to **sob**.

"I got lost!" I wailed. "I'm aloooooooone!
I was so foolish!"

It was useless. No one could hear me. I
would have to spend the night alone in the
wild forest.

But then a second later, the foliage
around the tree parted. A tiny face with a
ᴄᴜʀɪᴏᴜs expression peeked out
from between two leaves.

MY NAME IS COLIBRÌ!

The face belonged to a tiny mouselet. She wore a necklace of **shiny** red-and-black berries, and **MULTICOLORED** feathers were woven throughout her fur. Her **bright** eyes peered at me with a sincere and honest gaze.

She spoke to me in a language I didn't understand. When she saw my puzzled expression, she repeated it in Portuguese, and I understood.

"My name is **Colibrì**."

I smiled and replied in Portuguese.

"*O meu nome é* Stilton, *Geronimo Stilton*!"

Ana's **LESSONS** sure had come in handy! Colibrì smiled again and invited me to follow her. She started down a long path that took us **DEEPER** into the forest. We walked through the dense foliage by the light of the moon as my new friend proudly explained the secrets of that extraordinary natural habitat.

We walked and walked until we came to a small village in a clearing. It was very QUIET, and everyone was sleeping peacefully.

Macaw

Howler monkey

Jabiru

Tapir

Caiman

Capybara

Piranha

Toco Toucan

Anaconda

Jaguar

Caracara

THE PANTANAL is the largest tropical wetland in the world. Most of it lies within the Brazilian states of Mato Grosso and Mato Grosso do Sul. The name Pantanal comes from the Portuguese word *pântano*, which means *swamp* or *marsh*. During the rainy season in the Pantanal, the forest is almost fully submerged in water! A great variety of animal and plant species live in the Pantanal, making it one of the richest ecosystems in the world. For this reason, the Pantanal is considered a UNESCO World Heritage Site.

"Come out, everybody!" **Colibrì** suddenly shouted. "Geronimo has arrived!"

SLeePy mice began to emerge from the leaf-woven huts. They looked at me CURiOUSLY. I noticed that all were either very young or very old mice. How odd! Where were the adult rodents of the village?

A wise-looking elderly rodent came toward me.

"We have been waiting for you, Geronimo!" he exclaimed.

"You were waiting for me?" I asked, surprised. "Really? Why?"

"We have been waiting for you!" he repeated. "You are Geronimo, Wild Willie's friend, correct?"

"Is Wild Willie here?" I asked excitedly.

"No, but several days ago I received a LETTER from him saying you'd come to help us," he told me. "That's why we've been waiting for you."

I was PUZZLED. How could I help these mice? I asked for an explanation.

The old rodent led me to a spring of CLEAR water and began his story.

"Our people have lived in *peace* since the dawn of time. And since the dawn of time, our people have guarded our most precious **_treasure_**: The Heart of Light. It is a crystal shaped like a heart that emits the purest and most marvelous light. Unfortunately news of this wonderful crystal reached the ears of **Jake Darkmouse**. He's a dishonest rodent who's the leader of a band of ruffians. He and the scoundrels who work for him **_chop_** down trees in the forest to sell the wood. They replace nature with **CONCRETE** streets and buildings!"

"What happened to the Heart of Light?" I asked anxiously.

"One sad day, Jake Darkmouse came and asked to buy the CRYSTAL. He wanted to break it into **PIECES** to make souvenirs for tourists. We refused to sell it to him because the Heart of Light is part of our traditions."

"Jake Darkmouse didn't give up," the

Alas!

BORORO

The Bororo people are one of many indigenous populations in Brazil. The Bororo live in the state of Mato Grosso in villages that are made up of houses arranged in concentric circles. In their language, *Bororo* means "village court" or "round village." At the center of each village, there's a place where sacred ceremonies are held. This place is called *Baito*, which means "house of men." The Bororo typically adorn themselves with splendid multicolored headgear made of feathers.

rodent continued with tears in his eyes. "One night he and his thugs arrived with an **ENORMOUSE** helicopter, and they stole the crystal! They **CAPTURED** the rodents of the village who were trying to defend the Heart of Light. Darkmouse now keeps them as PRISONERS, forcing them to cut down trees!"

"How **terrible**!" I exclaimed. "Now I understand why your village is made up of only older mice and very young mouselets."

He nodded and then continued his story.

"A few weeks ago, I *wrote* a letter to my old friend Wild Willie and asked for his help. He has come to our defense several times before when we were faced with INJUSTICE. He replied and told me he would send *you*: a mouse named GERONIMO."

He looked at me carefully.

"You must be a mouse who's **VERY** strong, **VERY** cunning, **VERY** courageous, and also **VERY** adventurous. Jake Darkmouse and his henchmice are **VERY**, **VERY** bad rodents!"

DON'T HAMMER
THAT MOUSE!

I tried to correct my new friend.

"I hate to DISAPPOINT you, but I'm neither strong nor cunning," I told him SHEEPISHLY. "And I'm not at all adventurous! Most of all, I'm not COURAGEOUS! In fact, I'm a real scaredy-mouse."

"Don't be so MODEST!" answered the elderly mouse. "Wild Willie told us you would deny it, but I know the *truth*." He winked at me. "I know you're **the boldest, bravest mouse on Earth!**"

What could I do? He didn't believe me!

The rodent called Colibrì over, and she showed me to an empty hut and wished me a **good night**.

Heeeeeeelp!

Unfortunately, it was not a good night at all. It was the custom of the rodents in the village to sleep in **hammocks**. But when I tried to lay in mine, it flipped **UPSIDE DOWN**! I fell and bruised my tail.

Only after many painful tries did I finally figure out how it worked. In fact, once I got the hang of it, it was very COMFORTABLE! But unfortunately, I still couldn't **sleep**. I kept thinking of what the wise old mouse had said. I couldn't understand why Wild Willie had told him I was COURAGEOUS. But I had to *help* my new friends. I was their last hope, and I couldn't DISAPPOINT them!

At dawn, I gathered up my courage, said my good-byes, and headed in search of **Jake Darkmouse** and the **Heart of Light**.

Before leaving, I took Colibrì aside.

"I'll do the best I can, but I'm not sure I'll succeed," I whispered to her. "You've got to know I'm not what you think I am . . . **I'm just an ordinary mouse!**"

She smiled at me.

"Here's my advice," she said. "Have **FAITH**! You'll see that the **Forest** always helps those who **DEFEND** her!"

With those words in my heart, I entered the forest **ALONE**. I roamed for three days but found nothing. I got more tired and **HOPELESS** as I went. Then I remembered Colibrì's advice.

"I could use some help," I whispered.

Nothing happened. So I raised my voice

and repeated myself.

"I could use some **HELP**!" I said.

When nothing happened, I screamed as loud as I could.

"I really need heeeeeeeelp! Please help meeeeeeee!"

An instant later, something **TUGGED** on my sleeve. I turned and saw a monkey. It seemed to be pointing to a path in the forest.

Amazed, I began to **walk** along the path. When I came to a crossroad, I saw a tapir. It seemed to be pointing to the **left** with its snout, so I turned to the left. After walking a bit farther, I was sure I was lost. But then I saw a **MULTICOLORED** butterfly **swoop** in close. It fluttered its wings and moved toward a road. I began walking down the road, and a **YELLOW** armadillo crossed in

front of me, forcing me to bear right. Then a jaguar appeared before me and gave me a huge slap with its **paw**, putting me back on the right **track**!

I continued on until **sunset**, when I heard a tremendous metallic **noise**. I hid in the shrubs and peeked out into a clearing in the woods. I gasped. I was speechless! Bulldozers and tractors were **uprooting** trees, and an enormouse **GLIMMERING** crystal sat in the center of the clearing.

Suddenly, a large parrot landed on a branch above my head.

"Crrrrrrystal, crrrrrrystal, crrrrrrystal," the parrot squawked.

Then it disappeared into the forest. I was left hidden in the foliage, unsure of what to do. I peered into the clearing again, and singled out the mouse who seemed to be the boss. It had to be Jake Darkmouse! Holey cheese, I was SCARED just looking at him!

Then he spoke.

"I am personally going to be the first to break this huge crystal," he said loudly. "I'll use the first piece to make myself a souvenir keychain! Hee, hee, hee!"

He grabbed a huge HAMMER.

"Go, boss! Go, boss! Go, boss!" everyone around him chanted.

He wound up and was about to take a HUGE swing with the hammer. I had to do something! I had to defend the Heart of Light, no matter what! I put my fears aside, jumped out of the bush, and ran toward the CRYSTAL, throwing myself on top of it.

"You'll have to go through me to get to this CRYSTAL!" I cried.

I closed my eyes and waited. Suddenly, I heard a deep voice.

"Everyone, stop!" the voice shouted.

My eyes flew open. I knew that squeak! It was Wild Willie!

It was really him, in the fur. He did a karate

Go, boss!

Go, boss!

Ka-pow!

move as he **YELLED** at Jake Darkmouse.

"Don't **hammer** that **MOUSE**!" he cried. "I mean, don't hammer that CRYSTAL!"

Maya appeared behind Wild Willie. Before I could get over my surprise, she took out her whip and yanked the **hammer** out of Jake Darkmouse's hand!

Behind Maya, I saw a group of Bororos. It was the young mice from the village! Wild Willie and Maya had freed them! Jake Darkmouse realized he was *surrounded*.

"We give up!" he said. "You won!"

Crack!

"I saw the whole thing," Maya told me. "Geronimo, you were so **brave**!"

"Th-thank you," I stammered. My snout turned **purple** with embarrassment. Then I took a step backward and tripped over my own paws! How mortifying!

YOU CAME BACK
ALIVE, STILTON!

I returned to the village with Wild Willie and Maya, who carried the Heart of Light.

When we arrived, Colibrì ran out to GReet us.

"Geronimo is back!" she shouted. "And Wild Willie and Maya are here, too! They

have the Heart of Light! **HOORAY!**"

The head of the village came toward me and thanked us **FORMALLY**.

"**HOORAY** for Geronimo!" everyone shouted. "**HOORAY** for Wild Willie! **HOORAY** for Maya!"

Wild Willie, Maya, and I spent a few more days in the village, but soon it was time for us to go.

I bid my **FAREWELL** to my new friends.

"Thank you for everything," I told them in Portuguese. "I will never **forget** you. Come visit New Mouse City! I'll be happy to **host** you in the same wonderful way you hosted me!"

During our flight home, I went over all the Portuguese words and expressions I had learned during my incredible adventure. When the flight attendant wished me a good trip, I answered her in perfect

Portuguese. Ana's lessons had really made me look good!

When the plane landed in New Mouse City, my **family** was there to greet us — my sister Thea, my cousin Trap, and my **dear** little nephew Benjamin. Obviously, Bruce was there as well. He gave me his

Hi: Oi
Good-bye: Até logo
What is your name?: Como se chama?
How are you?: Como vai você?
Please: Por favor
Thank you: Obrigado/obrigada
You're welcome: De nada
Good morning: Bom dia
Good afternoon: Boa tarde
Good evening: Boa noite
Yes: Sim
No: Não

usual **CRUSHING** bear hug.

"Welcome home, **Cheesehead**!" he exclaimed.

Wild Willie and Bruce exchanged a knowing **GLANCE**.

"Incredible!" Bruce said as he smoothed his whiskers. "The greenhorn came back **alive**! Go figure!"

I was proud of myself.

"If you only knew all the adventures I lived through!" I told Bruce. "They were extremely **ADVENTUROUS** adventures! You wouldn't believe me if I told you! Unfortunately, I don't even have a single **photo**...."

Bruce winked at me.

"Don't worry about that, Cheesehead!" he said. "Here are the photos!"

"But . . . but . . . who took them?" I

stammered. "I was alone the entire time!"

Bruce knocked playfully on my head.

"Hello, is anybody there?" he asked.
"Haven't you figured it out yet? You were
never alone: Maya and Wild Willie were
with you all along!"

EXTREMELY ADVENTUROUS ADVENTURES

Clinging to the door of a speeding vehicle!

Eating piranha soup!

Freefalling over the Iguazu Falls!

Posing for a photo with a *jibóia*!

Hiking toward the Pantanal!

Spending time with new friends!

Saving the Heart of Light!

Knock, Knock, Anybody There?

I was stunned. Had all of my adventures been organized by my friends?

"But I — I mean, you — that is, we —" I stammered.

Bruce KNOCKED on my head again.

"Knock, knock, anybody there?" he asked. "We **abandoned** you on purpose so you could survive all on your own. You danced the samba, lived through the falls, ate piranha soup, and had a HUGE SNAKE around your neck! Aren't you at least a tiny bit grateful?"

Wild Willie chuckled as he stroked his whiskers.

"With all the effort we put in, of course

you should be thankful! A **rookie** like you could never have gotten such beautiful **ADVENTURE** photos all by himself! If I hadn't taken your wall —"

Bruce cut him off with a sharp elbow to the ribs.

"**Shhhhhhhhhhhh!**" Maya scolded him.

Suddenly, everything was **CLEAR** to me.

"You took my wallet and left me stranded in a **FOREIGN** country!" I shouted. "How could you do that to me? Some **FRIENDS** you are!"

Bruce **SLAPPED** me on the shoulder.

"Yep, Cheesehead, that's right!" he said with a chuckle. "And that makes us some of the **best** friends you'll ever have! We worked hard to make sure your **CHALLENGES** would be more exciting!"

Maya opened her laptop and turned the screen toward me.

"Check it out, Geronimo," she said. "Your new **Mousebook** page is up!"

The site appeared on the screen, full of the **adventurous** photos of me that my friends had taken during my trip. I also saw the comments that were beginning to **POUR** in from all over Mouse Island. They were from 𝒻riends and relatives,

and from **RoDents** who had read my books.

"*Congratulations, Geronimo!*"

"Well done, G!"

"I didn't know that you could be so ***courageous***, Geronimo!"

And: "You're really an **ADVENTUROUS** mouse, Geronimo!"

A little while later, my cell phone began to **ring**. My friends were all calling to compliment me on my **incredible** adventure!

I turned to my travel companions.

"Thank you for all you have done for me," I said sincerely. "I know you did it with the best **INTENTIONS** in the world, even if at the **moment** I didn't understand it. The result is **AMAZING**! My new Mousebook page is so much more **EXCITING** and bold than my 𝕭𝖔𝖗𝖎𝖓𝖌 old one! And thanks to all of you, I've discovered a *wonderful* country and made **fabumouse** new friends! This was a trip I'll never forget!"

GO FIGURE!

It was then I decided to write a **BOOK** about my Brazilian **adventure**. It's the book you're reading right now. I hope you like it!

Soon after the book was published, I received a phone call from the **FAMOUSE** Brazilian film director **OSCAR MOUSO**!

"*Senhor* Geronimo, I read your book and I liked it **a lot**. You showed what an adventurous country Brazil is!"

I thanked him for the **generous** compliment.

"So, *Senhor* Geronimo, what do you say about having the **LEADING ROLE** in a film based in Brazil?"

I was shocked.

"But . . . but . . . I'm not an actor!" I replied.

"Even better, *Senhor* Geronimo, even better!" he said with a chuckle. "I want **YOU**, only you, and just you, because you are a very **NORMAL** mouse who became a very adventurous mouse!"

And that's how I ended up **BACK** in Brazil filming a movie! The *best* part was that I got to see all my Brazilian friends again. When the film was done, there was a screening in New Mouse City. It was incredibly **SUCCESSFUL**!

I learned so many things from my adventure in Brazil. First of all, I learned that sometimes unfortunate event can turn out to be extremely fortunate! If I hadn't been left in Rio penniless, I never would have

Oscar Mouso

gotten to dance the SAMBA during Carnival! And I also learned that nothing is **IMPOSSIBLE** with the help of true friends. What would I have done without all those rodents who welcomed me with so much WARMTH and **hospitality**? Finally, I realized that real danger is not finding oneself with a snake around one's neck, but living a **boring**, monotonous life without ever trying anything **NEW**!

Luckily, I have some of the **BEST** friends in the world. Bruce Hyena, Wild Willie, and Maya knew what I needed even better than I did — an amazing adventure! Thanks for reading all about my **FABUMOUSE** trip to Brazil, and I'll see you next time!

Don't miss any of my other fabumouse adventures!

#1 Lost Treasure of the Emerald Eye

#2 The Curse of the Cheese Pyramid

#3 Cat and Mouse in a Haunted House

#4 I'm Too Fond of My Fur!

#5 Four Mice Deep in the Jungle

#6 Paws Off, Cheddarface!

#7 Red Pizzas for a Blue Count

#8 Attack of the Bandit Cats

#9 A Fabumouse Vacation for Geronimo

#10 All Because of a Cup of Coffee

#11 It's Halloween, You 'Fraidy Mouse!

#12 Merry Christmas, Geronimo!

#13 The Phantom of the Subway

#14 The Temple of the Ruby of Fire

#15 The Mona Mousa Code

#16 A Cheese-Colored Camper

#17 Watch Your Whiskers, Stilton!

#18 Shipwreck on the Pirate Islands

#19 My Name Is Stilton, Geronimo Stilton

#20 Surf's Up, Geronimo!

#21 The Wild, Wild West

#22 The Secret of Cacklefur Castle

A Christmas Tale

#23 Valentine's Day Disaster

#24 Field Trip to Niagara Falls

#25 The Search for Sunken Treasure

#26 The Mummy with No Name

#27 The Christmas Toy Factory

#28 Wedding Crasher

#29 Down and Out Down Under

#30 The Mouse Island Marathon

#31 The Mysterious Cheese Thief

Christmas Catastrophe

#32 Valley of the Giant Skeletons

#33 Geronimo and the Gold Medal Mystery

#34 Geronimo Stilton, Secret Agent

#35 A Very Merry Christmas

#36 Geronimo's Valentine

#37 The Race Across America

#38 A Fabumouse School Adventure

#39 Singing Sensation

#40 The Karate Mouse

#41 Mighty Mount Kilimanjaro

#42 The Peculiar Pumpkin Thief

#43 I'm Not a Supermouse!

#44 The Giant Diamond Robbery

#45 Save the White Whale!

#46 The Haunted Castle

#47 Run for the Hills, Geronimo!

#48 The Mystery in Venice

#49 The Way of the Samurai

#50 This Hotel is Haunted

#51 The Enormouse Pearl Heist

#52 Mouse in Space!

#53 Rumble in the Jungle

Up next!

#54 Get into Gear, Stilton!

Be sure to check out these exciting Thea Sisters adventures!

Thea Stilton and the Dragon's Code

Thea Stilton and the Mountain of Fire

Thea Stilton and the Ghost of the Shipwreck

Thea Stilton and the Secret City

Thea Stilton and the Mystery in Paris

Thea Stilton and the Cherry Blossom Adventure

Thea Stilton and the Star Castaways

Thea Stilton: Big Trouble in the Big Apple

Thea Stilton and the Ice Treasure

Thea Stilton and the Secret of the Old Castle

Thea Stilton and the Blue Scarab Hunt

Thea Stilton and the Prince's Emerald

Thea Stilton and the Mystery on the Orient Express

Thea Stilton and the Dancing Shadows

Don't miss these very special editions!

THE KINGDOM OF FANTASY

THE QUEST FOR PARADISE: THE RETURN TO THE KINGDOM OF FANTASY

THE AMAZING VOYAGE: THE THIRD ADVENTURE IN THE KINGDOM OF FANTASY

THE DRAGON PROPHECY: THE FOURTH ADVENTURE IN THE KINGDOM OF FANTASY

Check out my first hardcover!

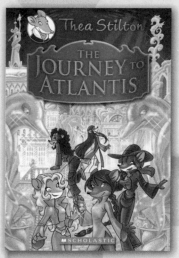

THEA STILTON: THE JOURNEY TO ATLANTIS

Meet
CREEPELLA VON CACKLEFUR

I, *Geronimo Stilton*, have a lot of mouse friends, but none as **spooky** as my friend CREEPELLA VON CACKLEFUR! She is an enchanting and MYSTERIOUS mouse with a pet bat named **Bitewing**. YIKES! I'm a real 'fraidy mouse, but even I think CREEPELLA and her family are AWFULLY fascinating. I can't wait for you to read all about CREEPELLA in these fa-mouse-ly funny and **spectacularly spooky** tales!

#1 THE THIRTEEN GHOSTS

#2 MEET ME IN HORRORWOOD

#3 GHOST PIRATE TREASURE

#4 RETURN OF THE VAMPIRE

Meet
GERONIMO STILTONOOT

He is a cavemouse—Geronimo Stilton's ancient ancestor! He runs the stone newspaper in the prehistoric village of Old Mouse City. From dealing with dinosaurs to dodging meteorites, his life in the Stone Age is full of adventure!

ABOUT THE AUTHOR

 Born in New Mouse City, Mouse Island, **GERONIMO STILTON** is Rattus Emeritus of Mousomorphic Literature and of Neo-Ratonic Comparative Philosophy. For the past twenty years, he has been running *The Rodent's Gazette*, New Mouse City's most widely read daily newspaper.

Stilton was awarded the Ratitzer Prize for his scoops on *The Curse of the Cheese Pyramid* and *The Search for Sunken Treasure*. He has also received the Andersen 2000 Prize for Personality of the Year. One of his bestsellers won the 2002 eBook Award for world's best ratlings' electronic book. His works have been published all over the globe.

In his spare time, Mr. Stilton collects antique cheese rinds and plays golf. But what he most enjoys is telling stories to his nephew Benjamin.

1. Main entrance
2. Printing presses (where the books and newspaper are printed)
3. Accounts department
4. Editorial room (where the editors, illustrators, and designers work)
5. Geronimo Stilton's office
6. Helicopter landing pad

THE RODENT'S GAZETTE

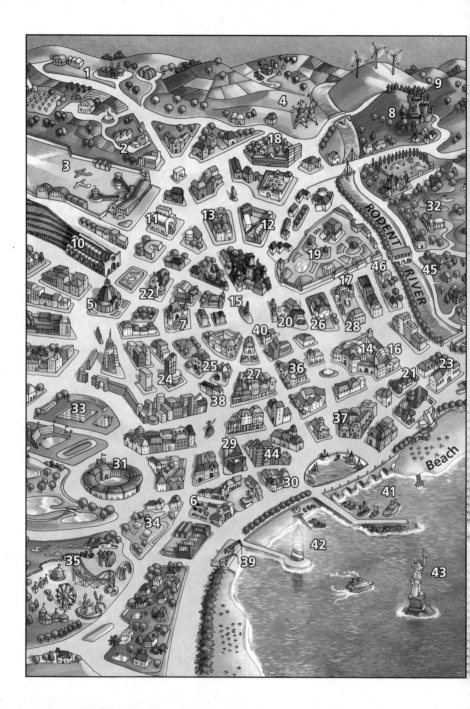

Map of New Mouse City

1. Industrial Zone
2. Cheese Factories
3. Angorat International Airport
4. WRAT Radio and Television Station
5. Cheese Market
6. Fish Market
7. Town Hall
8. Snotnose Castle
9. The Seven Hills of Mouse Island
10. Mouse Central Station
11. Trade Center
12. Movie Theater
13. Gym
14. Catnegie Hall
15. Singing Stone Plaza
16. The Gouda Theater
17. Grand Hotel
18. Mouse General Hospital
19. Botanical Gardens
20. Cheap Junk for Less (Trap's store)
21. Aunt Sweetfur and Benjamin's House
22. Mouseum of Modern Art
23. University and Library
24. *The Daily Rat*
25. *The Rodent's Gazette*
26. Trap's House
27. Fashion District
28. The Mouse House Restaurant
29. Environmental Protection Center
30. Harbor Office
31. Mousidon Square Garden
32. Golf Course
33. Swimming Pool
34. Tennis Courts
35. Curlyfur Island Amusement Park
36. Geronimo's House
37. Historic District
38. Public Library
39. Shipyard
40. Thea's House
41. New Mouse Harbor
42. Luna Lighthouse
43. The Statue of Liberty
44. Hercule Poirat's Office
45. Petunia Pretty Paws's House
46. Grandfather William's House

Map of Mouse Island

Dear mouse friends,
Thanks for reading, and farewell
till the next book.
It'll be another whisker-licking-good
adventure, and that's a promise!

Geronimo Stilton